THE PATIENT, THE DOCTOR AND THE BILL COLLECTOR

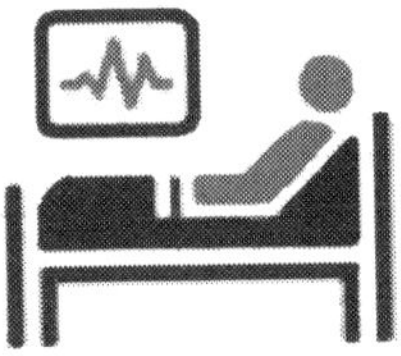

THE PATIENT, THE DOCTOR AND THE BILL COLLECTOR

An Obamacare and Medical Debt Collections Survival Guide

Robert E. Goff and Jerry Ashton

HOKU HOUSE
Kauai, Hawaii

THE PATIENT, THE DOCTOR AND THE BILL COLLECTOR

www.NoMoreMedicalDebt.com

Published by Hoku House
Kauai, Hawaii
HokuHouse.com

ISBN:
978-0-9892241-6-1 (hardcover)
978-0-9892241-8-5 (softcover)
978-0-9892241-9-2 (ebook)

Printed in the United States of America and overseas.

Cover and book design by 1106 Design
Book quality control by Judah Freed
Photo of Robert Goff by Jerry Ashton
Photo of Jerry Ashton by Brent Wise, MD

Publisher's Cataloging-In-Publication Data

The Patient, the Doctor and the Bill Collector:
An Obamacare and Medical Debt Collections Survival Guide

Goff, Robert (1952–)
Ashton, Jerry (1937–)

1. Personal Finance. 2. Business & Money. 3. Self Help/Success.
4. Medicine Economics. 5. Medical Practice Management
6. Medical Reimbursement. 7. Economics.

CONTENTS

THE PATIENT, THE DOCTOR AND THE BILL COLLECTOR

ACKNOWLEDGEMENTS

First, a joint acknowledgement on our part to the people essential to the creation of this book.

Within our industries, we acknowledge the role played in our education by professionals of the CureMD Corporation (billing) and MoneyQuest (collections). Both companies are leaders in their fields and the standard by which we judge their industry

Hands-down, the team of the Rolling Jubilee and Strike Debt win the "As Inspired By" award. Such gall they displayed — to think that medical debt should be abolished, and that people-bailing-out-people could be the mechanism! Occupy Wall Street would be considered a success had only this one organization emerged from the actions that started at Zuccotti Park.

Much appreciation to publisher Judah Freed of Hoku House for his patient counseling while he guided us to produce this book as a work of art as well as a work of thought. Thanks to Michele DeFilippo and Ronda Rawlins of 1106 Design for guiding us through the editorial process to ensure that the insides and outside of the book would appeal. A tip of the hat to Frank Kresen of Proof Positive for editing and endnotes.

Goff – In appreciation of my wife Jinny, for her continued love and support, and my son Blake, whose experiences with the healthcare system have provided me a very personal and different perspective. I owe much to the physician members of University Physicians Network whose "put the patient first" orientation caused me to truly appreciate the struggle of head and heart. Specific thanks go to Doctors Stuart Garay and Sol Zimmerman, whose continued guidance and personal leadership demonstrate the integrity to be found in the healthcare industry.

Lastly, in remembrance of the late Vincent Polito, my first employer in the healthcare industry at Waltham Hospital in Waltham, MA.

Ashton – The immediate and foremost recipients of my thanks are the wonderful women in my life. This includes my love and life partner, Kate, and daughters Andrea Ashton Norr and Alexandra Ashton Nemec. They and their families were my cheering squad long before this book and have since become great sounding boards. Not to forget my "main men," Craig Antico and Tony Bonifacic, with whom I have forged powerful partnerships over many years of working together. I am honored to work with Craig in the RIP Medical Debt project, and with Tony at MoneyQuest.

Here is where I must also thank two recently departed friends and colleagues in the sales and collections industry, Robert Hunter, founder of MoneyQuest and Allan Strucksberg, who founded the American Revenue Management collection agency in San Francisco's East Bay. Both men were as brilliant as they were colorful, and I miss their presence.

THE TIN MAN AND THE SCARECROW

Prologue — Goff

Two characters in *The Wizard of Oz* are the well-known Scarecrow and the Tin Man. The Scarecrow was missing a brain, and the Tin Man was missing a heart. Or so they thought.

The authors of this book had similar misperceptions in how we once viewed medical debt.

Jerry Ashton, with more than 40 years in collections, saw it as business, just business. You received a medical service or products, and now you must pay for it, even if you don't want to pay or can't. Stretching the Oz analogy, that appears heartless.

With more than 40 years in the healthcare industry, I took a traditional view: "If you want quality, it's going to cost. That's how it is." Stretching the analogy again, this appears thoughtless.

Our first meeting some years back was a pitch to me by Ashton to provide an automated medical debt collection service to physicians in my association, the University Physicians Network

(UPN). It was a good business proposition that was inexpensive to purchase and implement. I consented to having his service featured on my organization's website — the only collection approach that I could support or ever have.

Over time, over years, both of us evolved in our thinking.

As I labored in the healthcare industry, I saw that the medical community was torn between the need to generate revenue — a problem for the *head* — and compassion toward patients on whom they needed to institute debt collection — a problem for the *heart*. As Jerry toiled in collections, he grew to see that success in collecting was often a destructive process for the debtor. It was and is unsettling. He wanted to see that his clients got paid, but at what cost?

We spent hours across many months discussing and puzzling through the conflict of head and heart. We grew a desire to offer a different, more realistic yet compassionate perspective on medical debt. We needed to better understand how it is generated, its impact, and what would be needed to remedy the issue.

The journey to this book reflects that evolution in our thinking.

Initially, our approach was to identify existing resources of insurance, charity, governmental programs, and how to best educate people caught in the trap of choosing between their health and their wallet. However, when we stepped back and looked at the growing impact of healthcare costs, it was so staggering that we had to dig deeper and address the root causes. We determined not to simply rearrange the deck chairs on the Titanic.

This resulting book is one of "solution by understanding and engagement." The more our reader understands how easy it is for medical debt to become crippling and how destructive to individuals and families it has become, the more they can understand the need to engage — to come to the rescue of the physician as well as the patient — and put to rest both of their financial pressures.

We asked exactly why are medical costs so high? Who should be bearing these costs, and why? And how?

Health Reform vis-a-vis Obamacare did not end this national discussion or debate; it may even have exacerbated the problem. The Affordable Care Act is a valiant attempt to address pieces of the issue, but it ends up as a patchwork quilt that keeps no one warm — or protected — as we shall explain.

Like the Scarecrow, we cannot be empty-headed about this issue. Like the Tin Man, we must find and employ our heart. By harnessing the two powerful forces of *head* and *heart*, great solutions can and will emerge.

Let's get to work on this, beginning now.

DEBT IS THE ENEMY OF THE PATIENT, PHYSICIAN, HOSPITAL, AND STATE

Chapter 1 — Goff

Medical debt is not a private matter, impacting just the debtor. Medical debt is a burden on the patient as well as the family, caregiver, healthcare provider, and hospital. It is shared by the general public as well as by the State. Shall I count the ways?

> Medical debt is not a private matter

Medical costs get between the patient and their obtaining medical care when needed early on. "When should I go to the doctor?" is impacted by "Can I afford medical treatment?"

When this delayed care is finally sought, the costs are predictably higher and the outcome poorer. The financial consequences of more expensive care is such that an individual or family may become impoverished and require public medical financing assistance in the form of Medicaid or charity care assistance.

For the patient, Medicaid or any charity assistance is not an escape from the burden of medical debt or the financial consequences related to illness. Medicaid and other assistance usually come to the rescue only after the patient and their family have spent down: Family financial resources have been depleted by medical costs due to the absence of insurance or because of limitations in insurance coverage.

Medicaid assistance to patients thus impoverished comes as one of several taxpayer-funded social support programs. In fact, access to nearly all medical charity support comes only after a patient or family is deemed essentially insolvent and in poverty.

For caregivers, Medicaid and other charity arrangements are not an attractive pay source. Taxpayer resentment at the growing tax burden has caused Medicaid to be severely restrained in its level of reimbursements, and there is continued debate about whether or not the payments cover even the cost of providing services. Care though charity services is generally limited to public clinics and emergency-room episodic care.

Those with health insurance are well advised not to feel secure in their coverage. Since most health insurance is tied to employment, a family member's loss of employment due to accident or illness can quickly move a middle-income family into medically induced poverty.

For those who lose their jobs, a regulation called COBRA, named for the Consolidated Omnibus Budget Reconciliation Act, is designed to protect an individuals' ability to retain their employer-sponsored health insurance in the event of job loss, but COBRA coverage come at significant cost.

The now-unemployed can be required to pay up to 102 percent of their former employer's health insurance premium. Those injured to the point of disability, if they extend the term of COBRA coverage because of disability, may be required to pay even more — up to 150 percent of that health insurance premium during the extension period. *Voilà!* New candidates for Medicaid.

Medicaid is like any charity life preserver obtained for medical care going forward, and here is the first important point to digest. Medicaid does not address the debt accumulated prior to that person becoming a Medicaid or charity recipient.

This means that even when health is restored and a person is able to return to the workforce, they and their family remain liable for accumulated debt. When you are struggling to pay off these old bills, you skimp on taking on the expense of needed medication. According to The Commonwealth Fund Biennial Health Insurance 2012 report, in that year, 43 percent of adults, or 80 million people, said they had skipped or delayed getting needed healthcare or filling prescriptions because of the cost and their already strained budget.

This is an increase from 75 million people who reported such problems in 2010. More than a quarter (28 percent) of adults with a chronic health condition said they had skipped doses or not filled a prescription for their health condition because of the cost.[1]

Millions of people skip or delay needed healthcare

Putting it off is not a solution. Studies report that people who delay or forego medical care are significantly less likely to report having excellent or very good health status and had significantly lower quality-of-life scores when compared to people who never delayed necessary medical care. Think of this in terms of the impact on an affected individual as well.

According to the 2013 national survey: *Privately Insured in America: Opinions on Health Care Costs and Coverage,* which surveyed adults ages 18 to 64 with private health insurance, 19 percent don't go to the doctor when they are sick, and 18 percent go without preventive and recommended care.[2]

The savings by avoiding a cancer screening may result in the later identification of more advanced cancer illness, a classic "Pay me now or pay me later" scenario. If your condition is deemed too late for successful treatment, you may pay with your life.

Being wise enough to seek medical treatment — but not being able to pay that bill — creates its own set of costs.

As of 2012, 75 million people reported problems paying their medical bills, up from 73 million in 2010 and 58 million in 2005. An estimated 48 million people were paying off medical debt in 2012, up from 44 million in 2010 and 37 million in 2005.[3]

And When You Don't Pay Those Bills — Collections Start

Medical debt aggressively pursued is destructive of individual and family stability and security. Those without insurance coverage or with insufficient insurance coverage are pressured to make decisions between rent, food, transportation, and being a "responsible" person. To satisfy collection demands, those with limited financial resources may be forced to miss a mortgage payment or not put tires on their car.

> Aggressive medical debt pursuit is destructive

There is a greater urgency when the professional bill collector enters the picture. Their purpose is singular and direct: Collect monies owed their health-provider clients regardless of the consequences of the decisions they force debtors to make. The consequences can be grim.

Personal bankruptcies (the capital punishment of being a debtor), impacted two million people in 2013, according to a report by NerdWallet Health. This makes healthcare the #1 cause of bankruptcies, outpacing credit-card debt and unpaid mortgages. In addition, the report indicated that about 56 million adults — more

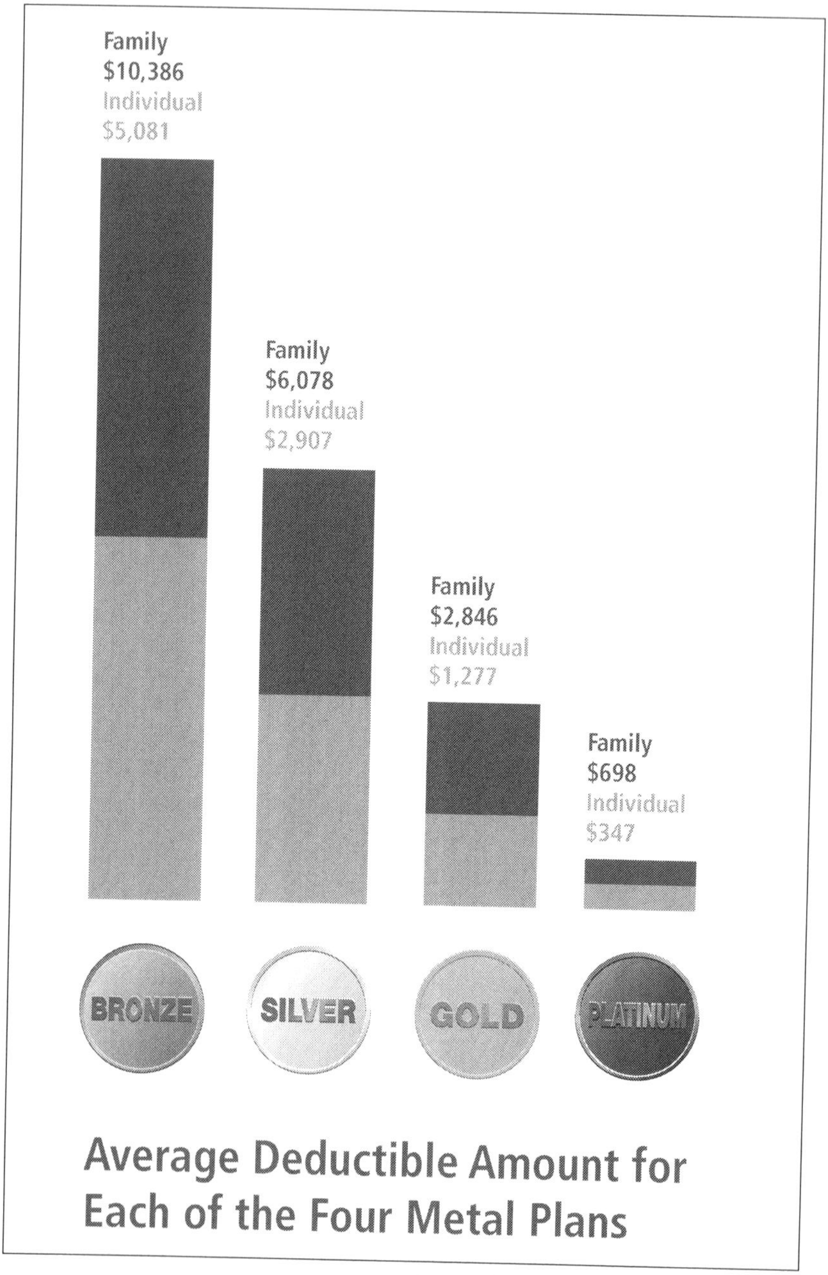

Source: Infostat, Healthpocket.com July 14, 2014

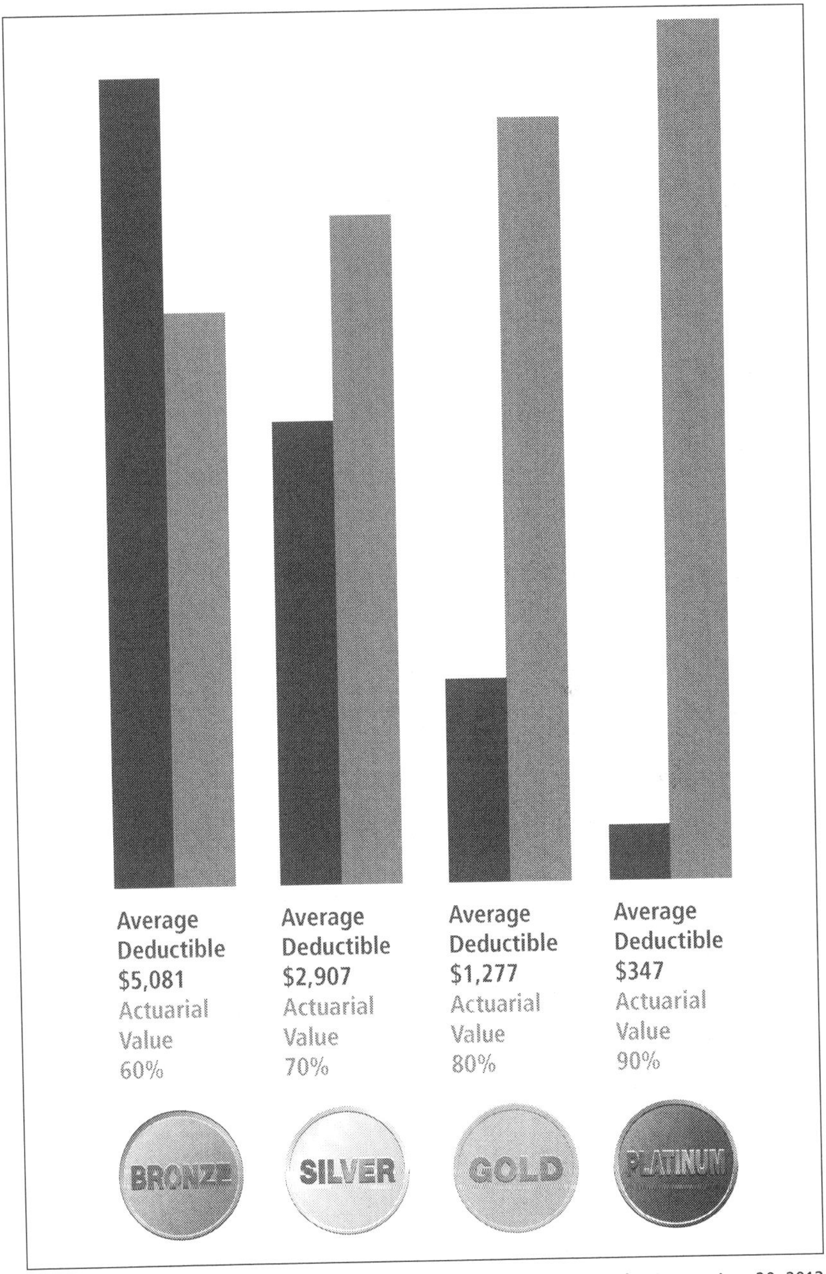

Source: Henry J Kaiser Family Foundation, 2013 Employer Health Care Benefits Survey, Aug. 20, 2013

than 20 percent of the population between the ages of 19 and 64 — will struggle with healthcare-related bills this year.[4]

The consequences of a personal bankruptcy remains with the released debtor for 10 years on their credit report, negatively impacting their ability to rebuild their lives as credit is denied to them. Also, you can forget about getting a mortgage. The enduring punishment of a personal bankruptcy, even after it is discharged, is that your slate is still not clean.

Adding to the injury, many employers now verify credit reports on prospective employees. The presumption is that individuals who are under personal financial stress or have difficulty managing their personal finances are more likely to commit white-collar crimes.

Not surprisingly, this further narrows job opportunities and with it, the earning opportunities for the debtor; it hurts the long-term financial stability of themselves and their families, causing their credit score to further deteriorate.

Those in poverty and the uninsured are not he only ones at risk of becoming a medical debtor. Many in the gainfully employed and insured middle class (what few remain) are at risk as well.

Employers Inflict Pain, As Well

As insurance premiums have increased, many employers have mitigated the costs by shifting them to the employee. Besides payroll deductions, more insidious has been the deterioration of benefits and coverage. These are often not understood until there is a medical crisis. In addition to rising co-pays, deductibles have increased, as have the maximum out-of-pocket costs for an insured individual.

According to the Kaiser Family Foundation, in 2013, for people with health insurance coverage through small business health benefits, deductibles had grown to under $2,000, and for those with coverage in large businesses, a little more than $1,100.[5]

Add to this exposure the "rules" of coverage.

Many insurance plans will refuse to pay for care, even when medically necessary, if it falls outside of their self-dictated restrictions. Examples are requiring pre-authorization for services or disallowing services provided by an out-of-network provider unless it qualifies as a life-threatening emergency. That definition can be subject to debate before an insurance company accepts responsibility to pay the bill.

Much to their detriment, Americans seldom invest the time needed to understand the nuances and limitations of their health insurance coverage. When they or a family member become ill, care is often sought without fully realizing the financial consequences from where and from whom care is sought.

Some medical providers are willing, for economic gain, to exploit this ignorance. (They are usually quite knowledgeable about their participation status with a patient's health plan or insurance and the rules or limitations of coverage even if they are not contracted to the carrier.)

A patient seeking to resolve even non-emergency needs can become enticed by such a provider to deliver that care. The same provider will profess total ignorance of the patient's coverage and will demand to be paid directly. This leaves the patient with greater economic exposure than if the patient had sought (or been counseled to seek) in-network care.

With no contract for participation with a health plan, the physician is not limited on what they charge. In some cases, the patient *and* their insurance carrier are exploited with unreasonable charges. The insurance carrier passes back these higher costs in higher premiums.

A common technique used by physicians, especially surgeons and other specialists not contracted with a patient's health insurance, is to ensnare patients with what is called "WIP" —*Whatever the Insurance will Pay*. Rather than lose the patient and the revenue, non-contracted physicians will offer to accept as payment in full whatever the insurance will pay.

Nasty surprise — a co-surgeon's $117,000 bill

The patient, now confident, proceeds to receive care and is up for an unwelcome and costly shock that often follows.

While the physician who "cut the deal" has agreed to accept WIP, no mention is made of the assistant surgeon or other assistants whom this physician invites to the procedure. Any assistant surgeons are not bound by any promise to the patient. In fact, the patient usually does not know who is assisting in the procedure. The nasty surprise, as was highlighted in a September 20, 2014, *New York Times* article for one patient, was a $117,000 bill for that assistant surgeon.[6]

Aetna, a national health insurance company, has taken an aggressive stance toward the enticement of patients into financial traps. In New York, they filed a lawsuit against two doctors. They asserted that Dr. Ramin Rak positioned fellow doctor Shuriz Hishmeh, who was out-of-network, to act as co-surgeon on procedures performed on Aetna patients.

The distinction was clear. Dr. Rak, an in-network physician, was paid $183,294 for his services, yet Dr. Hishmeh, out-of-network, was paid more than $1.1 million for his services. Worse, patients can be left liable for the cost of services above the carrier allowable rates.[7]

Caution Required: Physician-Owned Operations

Even when the insurance company steps up and protects the patient by paying the bills, the cost of the financial abuse in such out-of-network scenarios inevitably results in higher healthcare premium costs for all.

A limited number of physicians take advantage of patients when they participate with a health plan but the physicians then provide services in a *setting* that is not participating.

For example, a physician may be participating in the patient's health plan but influences the patient to have a procedure performed at the ambulatory surgery center — in which the physician just happens to have an ownership interest. The center is not participating and has no hesitation to bill an amount unfettered by contract limits. The difference can be quite dramatic.

A non-contracted ambulatory surgery center in NYC used by a contracted (participating) physician billed a patient with out-of-network insurance coverage of more than $42,000 for a procedure that the insurance company would have paid a contracted (participating) center about $3,000.

As for patients, they were subject to out-of-network deductibles of $3,000. Their in-network cost would have been $1,000. Here's the double jeopardy. The physician separately gets paid a professional fee for his or her services and as an owner of the ambulatory surgery center, enjoys a portion of the profits earned.

For the patient influenced or captured by a non-participating provider while receiving an otherwise covered treatment, the economic exposure can be tremendous. This can range from a higher deductible to higher cost sharing or even exposure to being solely responsible for the total outrageous bill. As Jerry Ashton can assure you, this is often followed by aggressive collection efforts on behalf of the non-participating physician by use of the external bill collector.

Hospitalized patients are often among the most victimized by out-of-network situations, often aided and abetted by the very hospital from which they sought care.

Once admitted to a hospital, a patient becomes nearly totally dependent on the institution's care structure for the medical care they receive. You become "a patient" — even reduced to a number — that occupies a bed for a relatively short time. During that time, you are subject to a care structure that often puts your economic health at risk.

Most people do not realize that hospitals do not control the health-plan participation of the physicians who are not their direct employees but to whom they grant the privilege of using the hospital for admitting and caring for patients — and that is the majority of physicians in community hospitals.

In this scenario, one or more of your caregivers is not contracted with your plan. The physicians who are called in to consult on your situation may not be participating. In one egregious example, $56,980 reportedly was billed for a 25-minute bedside consultation by a non-participating physician in a New Jersey hospital.[8]

A $56,000 bedside consultation

In some situations, hospitals make it worse for patients by contracting exclusively with certain physician groups for staffing arrangements at the hospital but put no requirements on those groups regarding their health-plan participation.

For example, it's common for a hospital to contract with groups of physicians to provide anesthesia services or staff the emergency department. The physician groups agree to provide 24/7 staffing in return for the exclusive right to provide those services. However, the hospital places no requirement on these groups to participate with the health plans, claiming that it is an independent business decision of the group.

Hospitals can grant monopolies — to great cost

By entering into these contracts, hospitals grant these groups monopolies over that service, and monopolies tend to act monopolistically and price accordingly, as in the case of a rotating group of cardiologists that interpret all EKGs at a hospital — but with no requirement that the physicians participate with health plans.

The result is financial risk to the patient while a captive of the hospital — kind of like being drawn and quartered.

The Peril of the Independent Physician

Even for medical providers that try to follow the rules, the structure of medical insurance and health-benefit coverage means that medical debt will result.

It's hard to find reliable information on the level of medical debt that physicians experience, since medical practices generally operate on cash-based accounting principles, recognizing income only when cash is received and expenses only when paid. There is no recognition of bad debt as an expense, and there are no central reporting requirements like there are with hospitals. Some studies indicate that bad debt can run between 5.9 percent and 14 percent of a physician's billings.

A report in 2010 from the Medical Group Management Association indicated that on a per-physician basis, bad debts averaged $12,480 for an individual primary care physician, rising to $27,077 for an individual surgical specialist.[9]

The publication *Health Affairs* estimated that in 2013 unpaid care by office-based physicians totaled $10.5 billion.[10]

In a 2012 survey, the Physicians Foundation found that 62 percent of physicians said they provided $25,000 or more every year in uncompensated care.[11]

In addition to the economic losses that cannot be recovered by higher fees paid by insured patients (because of health-plan and Medicare fee limits), physicians experience disruption to care and even loss of the patient.

A primary-care physician may recommend further specialty care, but a patient's financial condition may result in that care or recommended prescription going unfilled. The likely result is a sicker patient revolving back into the primary-care practice or ending up in a hospital emergency room, a much more costly setting.

Seeking to avoid the higher cost of more specialized care, the patient may even press the primary-care physician to provide a level of care beyond the scope of that physician's general training and experience. The physician may be put in the position of trying to provide *some* kind of care, even if not optimal, rather than have the patient go without.

Going to the Hospital, but Not Paying

In 2011, America's hospitals provided $41.1 billion in "uncompensated care" — services provided but never paid by patients or insurors. *Health Affairs* magazine reported that hospitals' total cost for uncompensated care in 2013 grew to $44.6 billion.

According the American Hospital Association, uncompensated care represented 5.9 percent of annual hospital expenses in 2013 — $1.8 billion more than in 2010. Since 2006, uncompensated care has increased by approximately 8 percent annually.[12]

The national average for hospital bad debt is 3.17 percent, 2.21 percent for charity, and 5.38 percent for total uncollectable accounts. The Southeast region of America had the highest percentage of total uncollectable accounts at 6.7 percent.[13]

In too many cases, medical debt surpasses the capability of a person's or family's ability to pay. As a result, many are driven to access public assistance in the form of Medicaid via state and county administered medical assistance programs for the poor. However, to obtain Medicaid benefits, the individual and family must have been driven below the poverty level.

Gratefully, if ironically, the medical bill will serve to do exactly that.

Medicaid assistance for the newly medically impoverished becomes a cost to the taxpayer — an ongoing one — because Medicaid coverage is only a financial safety net and does *not* assure ready access to care or continuity of care.

There is another cost of Medicaid to the patient: Becoming a "Medicaid Recipient." This is the actual description of a person receiving the benefits of Medicaid. The term "recipient status" carries with it all of the negative connotations of a person who is receiving something for doing nothing. It is considered a low status, and much of the treatment provided individuals by the healthcare bureaucracy is reflective of this lower status.

> Too rich for Medicaid; too poor to pay the medical bills

Medicaid is not a salvation for many who are impoverished by medical expenses. The rules for obtaining Medicaid require the impoverishment of the family, which for working, middle-class families takes a long time to reach.

Medicaid costs continue to grow and put pressure on the budgets of both counties and states. This cost grows despite Medicaid payment levels being constrained year after year — to the dismay of physicians. Finding participating physicians who will accept new Medicaid patients has become more and more difficult.

Medicaid is now one of the largest expenditures for state and county government, demanding in 2012 more than $416 billion in taxpayer support.[14]

Uncompensated care provided by hospitals also is not without costs to the taxpayer. That $44.6 billion in uncompensated care in 2013 are dollars that hospitals must seek to recover elsewhere. That elsewhere is you.

Restraints on hospital rates by Medicare and commercial insurance companies largely eliminate what's called "cost-shifting" (the strategy of raising prices on other customers to cover shortfalls in payments from those of limited means). Unfair? Perhaps.

Thus, a hospital's uncompensated care costs add to the financial pressure on that institution. The facilities most disadvantaged (no surprise) are those in areas where general economic conditions are weak, those that serve poor and near-poor communities.

The ripple effect of hospital closings

Most hospital closures attributed to unmanageable financial pressure occur in communities and neighborhoods that are less well-off economically. The ripple effect of this closure is not only loss of access to care but also the loss of a positive economic force for jobs.

In 2013, 18 acute-care hospitals closed their doors, all citing fiscal pressures as the reason or partial reason for their closure.[15]

The consequence of medical debt at a hospital is the deterioration of a hospital's ability to serve its community, expand services, or in some cases even meet payroll and continue to operate. The reflexive response has been to resort to state or municipal financial assistance to keep the hospital's doors open — another cost borne by the taxpayer.

Problematic as it is, physicians in private practice do not have the benefit of access to governmental funds that offset the costs of their bad debt. As this debt increases and the physician is unable to absorb the revenue loss, hard decisions must be made. The responses to excessive medical bad debt are several; none are pleasant.

Rarely do physicians disengage from a patient over a financial issue. By law and custom, a physician cannot abandon a patient under active care, even if it means providing uncompensated care until the patient can find (or be placed with) an alternative caregiver.

Patients with outstanding financial obligations to the physician may be discharged early from the practice, disrupting care and its coordination. This discharge is often self-imposed, as the patient is embarrassed to owe money to their caregiver and quietly stops making and keeping appointments.

At other times, the physician, knowing the patient's economic hardship, refers the patient to another medical resource such as a community health center or public clinic.

There is a stark financial reality here: Physicians need to generate a certain level of revenue to support themselves and their operations. Because physician rates are fixed and time has already been expended for care, bad debt comprises dollars that cannot be replaced by increasing revenue elsewhere.

The result is often an unfortunate but understandable increased aggressiveness in a practice's collection efforts that destroy a physician-patient relationship and add to the stress of the patient.

In the extreme, medical debt can result in physicians closing and relocating their practice out of the community they served, not from a callous desire to abandon the community, but out of survival. Medical debt contributes to the mal-distribution of physicians and physician access in our communities.

Is this what America wants? It certainly isn't what Americans need.

Why Change is Needed

Below is the first of 11 emails requesting financial help by individuals who had seen a television interview in which the purchase and abolition of unpaid medical debt was discussed. They are someone's friend, neighbor, or family member.

Story #1

> *My son...has MS...released (from the hospital) to the tune of $30,000+ in medical bills...He now has no credit, can have no property in his name, has been hounded and pursued by creditors for over 3 years, and still makes only $12.00 per hour. This has been a nightmare for all of us, but for a grown man with pride, impossible.*[16]

AWAKENING TO A DEBT HANGOVER

Chapter 2 — Ashton

"I will apply all measures for the benefit of the sick according to my ability and judgment; I will keep them from harm and injustice."

FROM THE HIPPOCRATIC OATH, STILL SWORN TO BY DOCTORS GRADUATING FROM MANY MEDICAL SCHOOLS

Whatever your situation, interest or pedigree, it is safe to say that you could benefit from a keener insight into medical debt. It has an impact on you and your family (and society). Current solutions do not appear to manage or eliminate this scourge — all of which underscore the importance of keeping a *survival manual* at hand. The bank account you save may be your own.

I am in the business of collecting debt. I have been for more than 40 years. In lay terms, I am known as a "bill collector." That is not the whole picture of my professional history and my work experience, but I'll accept it as a fair description so that you can better evaluate the grounding of what I have to share.

Allow me to make a guess or two about you. If you are reading this book, you may likely fall into one of the following categories:

1. A person or a family who owes or anticipates owing medical debt and would like to know how to deal with it — and especially with those pesky people who pursue that debt.

2. A member of the medical industry who wants to know how to deal more effectively with patients who pay slowly or pay only some of a bill, plus when and how to seek outside help.

3. A member of the debt-collection industry who wants to stay aware of any changes or threats to your business or livelihood (such as the militant or better-educated debtor reading this book).

4. A member of the government, perhaps a legislator or even a lobbyist, and you are doing your best to find alternative ways for improving (or dismantling, if your political agenda so dictates) the ACA.

5. Someone who has an active — dare I say "activist" — interest in correcting the abuses of the collections and medical industries as well as insurers and governmental agencies.

Do you see yourself in one of these definitions? Well, even though you have selected this book as a perfect resource, expectations need to be set. Who you are, where you live, the laws in your state, and the protections available are all so individual as to boggle the mind. Even so, certain rules will apply, and certain solutions will seem almost tailor-made to your need to survive everyone's worst nightmare — to be sick, broke and hounded by the bill collector.

> Sick, broke and hounded by the bill collector

I have a lot to tell you about that, having been that voice on the other end of the telephone line for so many years. Just knowing how to talk to me and deal with me will give you an undeniable edge.

When I started in the debt collections industry in California in the late 1970s, it was as a salesman for a company that had developed a "receivables management system" for businesses that had problems collecting their overdue accounts.

My employer at that time was Transworld Systems. TSI then was a fledgling company that marketed a "receivables management" package to appeal to smaller businesses with only occasional incidents of debt.

I sold this service down the street, door-to-door, commission only. It was lucrative for me for many years. The experience provided me with a real-world education that served me well in my personal and professional growth. It helped me build a successful consulting and outsourcing business in accounts receivable controls, credit, collections, and customer service.

To say that medical practices were this company's favorite target would be an understatement. The doctor was akin to other mom-and-pop enterprises and equally unsophisticated in the pursuit of past-due or troublesome accounts. The doctor was not about to pick up the phone to chase down a bill, and the practice's bookkeeper or office manager were little better equipped.

Physicians needed all the help they could get. I was there to provide it, and I began to specialize in meeting and understanding their needs.

Doctors are prize prospects

Doctors are prized prospects — and great customers. They have an ever and ongoing problem with getting paid on time. It seems a truism that the doctor's bill is the last to be paid. Doctors are saddled with the costs of mailing out statements month after month that never seemed to be opened. Phone calls from their office staff asking about payment are only reluctantly returned. All too often, their bill will be at the bottom of the stack of unpaid bills on the family's kitchen table.

The physician was not my only medical-related prospect. Also unpaid were the x-ray services, the pharmacy, laboratories, home care, outside specialists, and the hospital or medical center. Oh, and the credit card companies, where patients ran up a fortune on expenses not covered by insurance.

TSI's service was effective. In comparison to internal collection pursuit costs, TSI was relatively inexpensive. Billing itself as a "letter service" for a fixed fee of only $3.95 per debtor assigned (sold in packages of 100), Transworld contracted to mail out five computer-generated contacts demanding payment on their agency letterhead to the errant debtor. This was one of the first instances of automation used in the collections industry.

If those five contacts failed to recover the money, the account was then transferred to a division of the company, CMS (Credit Management Services), which worked on a strict percentage basis and more aggressively pursued the debt.

Very aggressively.

Transworld, once owned by industry behemoth NCO Group[1] as Green Flag Profit Recovery, has been launched under new owners as "TSI" and retains the same business model.

The Importance of Medical Debt to the Collections Industry Today

For the collections industry at large, medical debt is a key component in their portfolio management. Fully 50 percent or better of the work done by the average collection agency nationwide is related to medical debt.

Starkly put, if medical debt were to disappear overnight, so would a significant percentage of America's collection agencies. Credit card statements would be slimmer for many people, as well.

Don't plan on that happening too soon. There's a lot of education that needs to take place, and a lot of changes will be required in the way things are seen and held (read: political will). Mostly, that change needs to start with *you*. The book you are holding is part of this education.

Yes, my fellow Scarecrow, we are asking you to employ your mind. Educate yourself, and then put that education to work! There are short-term tools and approaches you can put to work to answer your immediate needs, but it is in the broader understanding where you can transfer that knowledge to fuel personal and larger campaigns that can make a difference for everyone.

If Robert Goff and I succeed in our quest to equip you to better understand medical debt and the pitfalls of today's healthcare system, it will be done only in partnership with you and your willingness to seriously take on this subject. Only out of this partnership can any action on your part be guaranteed to bear fruit.

> You have to seriously take on this subject

This means you. It means the doctor and the hospital and the caregivers. It means the collections industry. It means the debt buyers and sellers. Any participant not willing to work toward reducing or eliminating medical bad debt must be seen for what they are — the problem.

Medical debt is no more than a subset of a world that lives on and profits from debt. Understand medical debt as being the *microcosm* with which we need to cope. We also live and deal with *macrocosm* of larger debt, which also needs to be understood and managed — and hopefully, dismantled.

As you will learn from Robert Goff, medical needs and costs can stagger — and even destroy — the financial well-being of the individual, family, medical practice, the hospital, and even the community served. Given the impact this has on the family as well as the national budget, *everyone* has a stake in this game. Regrettably, our national goals and purposes are not aligned — not yet. I refuse to believe that they will never be aligned.

The effort required to understand medical-debt issues may well bring on a headache or two. Breaking a path into unexplored territory is laborious, but that is a small price to pay for becoming aware and responsible. You *do* need to understand the Big Picture to accomplish this, and you *will* when you finish this book.

The Shame of it All is That There is Shame at All

Your first lesson.

One of the first things someone needs to comprehend and to integrate into their psyche is that it is not a disgrace to be in debt or to default on a debt. It may be unfortunate, regrettable, even stupid, but not a disgrace. Bad things happen to good people to put them behind the 8-ball, but do not allow your creditor to employ manipulative guilt and shame to collect on a debt.

> Shame is a bill collector's leverage

Creditors will do exactly that, worldwide. Debt collectors use guilt and shame as levers to pry money from debtors. The shame of it all for debtors is that there is any shame to start with; we are such gulls of the system. Even as victims of the system, we join in the chorus of blame.

Shame is a powerful tool of creditor and collectors. In my opinion and experience, shame is a manufactured emotion that is part of their collection strategy. "Shaming" is a very integral element in the manufacturing of debt and ensuring that this debt is paid.

Isn't it a bit odd that no shame — ever — is put on the villains who just might be perpetrating the debt scheme?

When was the last time you saw your banker shamed by a "perp walk" for their role in bringing about a worldwide economic collapse? When was the last time you saw a credit card company shamed for charging usurious interest rates and piling on exorbitant fees for "late payment" or "over limit?" They are enjoying two-martini lunches not to drown their guilt for aiding and abetting that condition, but to salute your victimhood.

When was the last time you heard of an attorney shamed for using robo-signed affidavits to force a homeowner into foreclosure? When was the last time you read about a bill collector shamed for using near-extortionate language to manipulate a debtor into paying a debt that, in itself, was questionable in nature? As for the payday lender, where is the shame or guilt on their part for saddling people with interest rates as high as 600 percent?

How many politicians will profess their shame for signing into law usurious interest rates and penalties or allowing questionable and overly aggressive business practices to suck the economic blood out of people? These are the same people who voted them into office.

You likely never will. It's how the game is rigged.

Consider the public shaming license given debt collectors in Spain as reported by Slashdot.com, "Debt collectors are using public shaming to get their money, including … sending a man in a tuxedo and top hat who follows you around everywhere and men dressed up like superheroes who ask your neighbors to help you out of your bad financial situation. One of the biggest collection agencies, *El Cobrador del Frac*, which translates to 'The Debt Collector in Top Hat and Tails,' employs more than 250 shame collectors."

Humiliation and fear

In the United Arab Emirates (UAE), a number of Indian expatriates working in the notoriously poor-paying public sector have committed suicide when pursued by that country's debt collectors. *The National World* reported:

> Humiliation and fear are crucial to keeping borrowers in line. The tactics include menacing phone calls, sending thugs to terrorize family members in India, and the threat of public shaming by showing up at the borrower's home and workplace.[2]

Don't believe for one moment that similar tactics wouldn't be used by people enforcing the payment of debt in the US, if they could get away with it. There have been cases in several states in which school cafeterias snatch meals away from children whose parents have not paid their lunch debts.[3]

And then there's the United States of America. In what is truly a shared shame, our government is the biggest debtor of all.

As defined by the U.S. Treasury, there are two calculations for debt. "Debt Held by the Public," which are U.S. Treasury securities held by institutions outside the United States Government, and "Gross Debt," which includes intra-government obligations, such as the Social Security Trust Fund.

On June 30, 2014, debt held by the public was approximately $12.6 trillion, or about 74 percent of Q1 2014 GDP. Intragovernmental holdings stood at $5.1 trillion (30 percent), giving a combined total public debt of $17.6 trillion, or about 104 percent of Q1 2014 GDP.

As of January 2013, $5 trillion — approximately 47 percent of the debt held by the public —was owned by foreign investors, the largest of which was the People's Republic of China and Japan, at just a little more than $1.1 trillion each.

I often wonder what their bill collectors are going to do about this. Will they hire subsidiary agencies or attorney collection firms here in America? Will they attempt to foreclose on the White House? Repo Air Force One? Put an agreed-upon percentage of our citizens in a Chinese gulag debtor's prison?

Our national debt hovered at $18,150,604,277,751 in October, 2015.[4] This adds up to almost $50,000 per citizen, or $154,000 per taxpayer. I believe that this totals about 104 percent of our GDP. The debt likely is higher when you read this paragraph.

At the time this book was being pulled together in early 2015, these were the debt statistics:

- *U.S. National Debt:* $18,152,809,942,589.
- *Household Debt:* $11,850,000,000,000.
- *Mortgage Debt:* $8,170,000,000,000.
- *Consumer Debt:* $2,680,388,392,000.
- *Student Debt:* $1,200,000,000,000.
- *Credit Card Debt:* $3,340,000,000,000.
- *Debt Per Capita:* $54,717.00.
- *Debt Per Taxpayer:* $154,161.00.

Check out this "Debt Clock" — www.usdebtclock.org — and see the wheels fly by, moving higher and higher and higher.

Being Free and Being in Debt are Mutually Exclusive

As above, so below.

We are indentured citizens of a debtor nation, which tells you a lot about how free and sovereign that makes us. How did this happen? Is medical debt in a category of its own, or is all debt inter-related? What does my $50,000 medical bill have in common with someone's $50,000 school loan? Or a $50 water bill in Detroit?

Using medical debt as our immediate teacher, we will be better prepared either to bear this yoke more easily or to free ourselves from it totally. It will be about equipping ourselves not just to survive this economy but to thrive in it and to see that our fellow citizens share in the solutions that will emerge.

At what point in time does a person confronted with what appears to be unfair and illegitimate and intractable circumstances throw up his or her hands and say, "Enough is enough!"?

When it comes to debt, for those heeding the lessons contained in this book, the answer will be: *Now!* An education in the origin and understanding of medical debt is a damned good start.

Why Change is Needed

Story #2

> *Since my mom's 2 strokes we have been piled up with bill after bill. My dad...is the only one paying bills and we lost our house because we weren't able to pay mortgage, we now live in an apartment which is also difficult for him to pay rent. I'm not writing for myself but I am asking to see if you could possibly help us out especially my dad to pay at least something from my mom's medical bills.*[5]

CONFLICT OF HEAD AND HEART

Chapter 3 — Goff

There is little sympathy for physicians — and greatly diminished respect and stature — in the current political and economic environment. Fair or otherwise, in the near-relentless drumbeat of criticism of the medical system and structure in America, physicians are garnering their share.

While there remains a level of trust between individual physicians and their patients, the profession has been painted or spattered with the ills and evils of the healthcare system. To add to the insult, physicians are now lumped into the disdained "One Percenters" and more often viewed as exploiters rather than contributors.

What is often overlooked is that physicians, as Jerry points out, in actuality are small business men and women.

Yes, there are the mega-physician groups and those physician practices that are owned by hospitals, but the majority of the frequent medical care that people receive is largely provided by individual physicians in small practices.

A 2012 survey of physicians by the American Medical Association shows that, while there has been a shift toward hospital employment, 53.2 percent of physicians were self-employed, and a full 60 percent of physicians worked in practices that were wholly owned by physicians. Only 23 percent of physicians worked in practices that were at least partly owned by a hospital, and another 5.6 percent were directly employed by a hospital.[1]

> The self-employed physician touches more lives

Looking further into the data, you find that the physicians who most frequently touch the lives and well-being of patients are the self-employed and physician-owned practices of family practitioners, internists, obstetricians/gynecologists, and those in internal medicine subspecialties.

According to an AMA study in 2008, the median number of employees per physician is six — four administrative/clerical (receptionists, billers, schedulers) and two clinical (nurses, medical assistants). It could be estimated that the 835,000 (2012) practicing physicians employ more than 5 million individuals.[2]

Physicians, in addition to their responsibilities for the delivery of medical care, must also endure all of the pressures and concerns of the small business owner. This includes payroll, rent, supplies, computers and specialized software programs, telephone, and the one expense for which other business owners do not have to budget — malpractice insurance.

The source of their revenue is the sale and delivery of professional expertise, specialized knowledge, generally sold in units of time — and time is a finite resource.

An online video titled *The Vanishing Oath,* directed by Ryan Flesher, MD, gives some sense of the financial realities of the "average" physician.[3]

The average physician salary in the United States is $146,000, which, at three times the national average for household income, is undeniably a lot of money. However, the video makes a near-startling point. When you factor in the overhead that physicians incur and the hours worked, the take-home pay of a physician today averages less than $28 an hour. Not a princely sum.

The average cost of the more than 200 million visits paid by Medicare in 2012 was just $57 — less than a plumber bills to fix a broken toilet, says Nancy Nielsen, MD, PhD, a past president of the American Medical Association.[4]

A lot is said about the burden of medical-education debt for physicians, and it is a factor in a physician's life. It influences where and how a physician chooses to practice. For example, if a physician is carrying medical-education debt, the choice of *where to practice* may be dictated more by the chance of paying off that debt than where the need is greatest.

In communities or neighborhoods where the population is economically challenged, private-practice physicians are in short supply. Costs cannot be met with a high volume of low-paying Medicaid patients without delivery quality suffering.

Physicians Follow the Money

This is why physicians tend to congregate in higher-income suburbs and the more upscale neighborhoods of cities. Selection of where to practice is about lifestyle and economics, not necessarily the needs of the population.

Also, the physician with high medical-education debt may choose to work on salary for a hospital, as opposed to private practice. The growth of the numbers of employed physicians is generating a separate debate about implications for access as well as control of medical care.

Medical debt influences not only where physicians practice but also who chooses to enter the practice of medicine. The compassion-oriented individual of modest means who would like to serve in rural and underserved communities has to confront the realities of paying for their medical education costs.

Medical-education debt, averaging $169,901 for medical-student graduates in the class of 2013, is very different from earning a four-year diploma or even the debt incurred to open a business.[5]

Traditional businessmen may invest $170,000 to open their doors, with no guarantee of drawing in a customer. MDs do not face that problem. Given the shortage of physicians, a medical license is a near-guarantee of income. Even if a doctor were not successful in his or her own small practice, that medical license is a near-surety of employment in clinics or hospitals for their entire working career. The investment in a medical education is well returned.

The great challenge to physicians when it comes to income is that the low valuation placed by Americans on healthcare compared with its costs. Physicians are an easy target for efforts to control costs, ignoring the fact that they are on the receiving end of bureaucratic burdens that are alleged to improve quality. In general, healthcare costs are perceived as too high and the quality too low. And the patient satisfaction/customer service level? Even lower.

> Physicians are easy targets

Unlike other small businesses, physicians' income is largely fixed and even out of their control. While business must adapt their prices to competition, physicians have the prices of their services dictated to them. Medicare establishes fixed rates paid to physicians for seniors, the largest consumers of healthcare services, and physicians agree to participate with commercial health plans in exchange for established rates.

Despite the perennial threats that physicians make that they will abandon participation in Medicare, figures from the Centers of Medicare and Medicaid indicate that better than 90 percent of practicing physicians participate in Medicare or accept Medicare

Year-to-Year Comparison of Average Commercial Reimbursements

Source: "Physician Reimbursement Dropped Sharply," *Physician's Money Digest,* February 02, 2013

patients. Some 69 percent participate with Medicaid. These numbers have held relatively steady over the years.[6]

Participation in commercial insurance plans has actually been increasing as health-benefit coverage is shrinking — and often even eliminated — for services provided by physicians that are not contracted to participate with commercial plans. For those that are participating with health plans, carriers have been less than generous in sharing their increasing premium income with physicians over the last ten to twelve years. Their payment rates to physicians are largely stagnant or declining.

Since 2001, pay rates to physicians have declined or remained flat for almost every year; however, cuts in 2012 were particularly steep, as a third of payers' health plans cut pay for services and began to experiment with new payment models. The trend likely will continue, too.[7]

Payments to physicians from commercial payers now run less then Medicare. Between 2006 and 2013, payments dropped by about 43 percent. Payment for the most common office visit is now calculated at 39.8 percent less than what Medicare pays. As the chart on page 38 shows, rates for office visits have been declining. (Medical code 99211 is a simple office visit, 99215 is the most complex visit, and 99213 is the most frequently occurring visit.)

A primal fiscal truth bears repeating: Physicians sell their time, and their time is a limited resource.

As costs of operating their business increase, reimbursements (constrained income for the physicians) are falling behind the increases in the costs they incur to be in business.

From 2002 to 2012, Medicare fee-for-service (FFS) rates increased 9 percent, while the cost of operating a practice — as measured by the Medicare Economic Index (MEI) — increased

27 percent, according to a recent report by the Medicare Payment Advisory Commission (MedPac). The MEI includes everything from physician and staff compensation to rent, exam-room tables, postage, and computers. During that same period, the overall inflation rate was 33 percent.[8]

Insurers Preying on Physicians?

While revenue is being squeezed and expenses are increasing, a number of health insurance companies are trying to make money from payments to physicians under the guise of "increasing administrative efficiencies." For example, a subsidiary of the national insurer Aetna is trying to pay physicians via pre-paid credit card. They are paying the contracted rates, but for the physician to cash in their pre-paid card, there is now a transaction fee.

The companies issuing the pre-paid cards are happy to offer that transaction fee to the employer and the insurer for a bit of profitability on the back of the physician. Aetna is not alone in trying this gambit.

Aetna has another subsidiary that is trying out a new technology to help their enrollees choose physicians. Called WellMatch, it allows patients to see which physicians are in the plan and what it will cost at that practice. For doctors, Aetna is proposing to sell them "preferred placement" on the lists for $200 a month.

United Healthcare offered a clever payment arrangement to physicians: Accept payment from your patients by credit cards for their portion of the bill by electronic funds transfer, through a company called InstaMed, for a fee higher than that charged by many credit card merchant service vendors.

But wait! If the physician does not agree to be manipulated into this business arrangement, as part of the deal it cut with InstaMed, United will automatically enroll them in another InstaMed program in which the physician is paid by a one-time-use paper credit card. Physicians will now have to pay to have this card processed in order to get their money. While physicians can get out of this arrangement, which they did not freely choose to participate in, United requires them to personally write United a letter pleading to opt out.

Physicians face intractable challenges

The doctor is moving from being a participating physician in health plans to becoming a source of revenue — ironically increasing the physicians' cost of doing business and enriching the already-too-fat insurer. Insurers extract their pound of flesh, coming and going.

The Dilemma of *Head vs. Heart*

The physician-patient relationship is unique as a business model. The physician, as a caregiver, is expected to provide specialized knowledge — and do it with a high degree of compassion. For the most part, the vast majority of physicians do. That is the source of a large part of his or her unique challenge as a businessperson.

Physicians are faced with an intractable challenge when it comes to maintaining their business and their practice, compensating the people they employ, and deriving a decent income.

On one hand, self-preservation requires that physicians get paid. This is crucial today as the financial solvency of medical practices is being threatened. Alternatively, there is a tradition of compassion on the part of the doctor, based on intimately knowing the patient-now-debtor. That connection with their patients is what causes many physicians to write off balances, to their own detriment.

No physician has ever joined a health plan because it was lucrative. Joining a health plan as a participating physician limits one's compensation and subjects one to the administrative burdens that come with health-plan rules and procedures.

Healthplans: An expensive gateway to helping patients

Physicians join health plans and insurance arrangements largely to support their patients. Their participation enables the patient to obtain the maximum coverage under their health and benefit programs, with fewer dollars coming directly from the patient's own pocket. Plan participation was seen as a way to stay focused on the patient-physician relationship for professional care by limiting the financial pressures of the relationship.

According to the study of colleagues by Lawrence P. Casalino, MD, Ph.D., of Weill Cornell Medical College, physician practices report that the overall costs of interacting with insurance plans is $31 billion annually, totaling 6.9 percent of all U.S. expenditures for physician and clinical services.

On average, physicians spend three hours a week, or nearly three weeks per year, interacting with health plans. Nursing staff spent more than 23 weeks per physician per year, and clerical staff spent 44 weeks per physician per year interacting with health plans. More than three in four respondents said the costs of interacting with health plans have increased over the past two years.[9]

According to a report by the Robert Wood Johnson Foundation, in March 2010, the cost to a physician of that administrative burden (in time, staff time, and resources) was more than $64,000 for a primary care physician and more than $78,000 for a specialist. No physician finds this burden a good use of time; it could better be given to patients and their care.[10]

In a 2012 survey, the Physicians Foundation found that doctors spend more than 22 percent of their time on non-clinical paperwork.[11]

Health-plan participation grew rapidly in the early days of Managed Care, when the cost of a patient-physician encounter was a low co-payment. Back in the early and mid-1980s, the patient's financial responsibilities to a physician were as low as $2 and $3 a visit. Even if the co-pays weren't collected, the impact was nominal. The patient-physician financial exchange was limited, nominal, and had no large impact on either party.

For those with limited or no insurance coverage, there has always been a higher level of intensity about the patient-physician financial arrangement. For many years, physicians could take a kinder, gentler approach as reimbursements from health plans and Medicare were rising at a rate comparable to the cost increases in operating a practice. What physicians might have lost on a write-off of a patient bill could more readily be absorbed in income from better-paying patients and plan reimbursements.

Now, with reimbursements fixed, and with some pay sources reduced and expenses increasing, such cost-shifting has been largely eliminated.

Even for those with insurance coverage, the patient-physician financial exchange is undergoing major change. Low co-pays and limited deductibles, if any, are disappearing. It's projected that patient responsibilities by the end of 2015 could easily reach 30 percent of the cost of care. Origin, a healthcare-analytics company, has reported that the patient financial responsibility for insured individuals has increased 47 percent since 2009, and now up to 40 percent of revenue is at risk due to patient bad debt.

Adding to the Intensity: Obamacare

Healthcare reform, known as the Affordable Care Act (ACA), only adds to the intensity of the patient-physician financial exchange.

In the debate about healthcare reform and the goal of getting health insurance for all Americans, there was little said about what it would cost to obtain that coverage.

Yes, there was much talk about premium costs and how there would be tax credits for businesses to provide coverage and subsidies to provide for individuals to purchase coverage, and there was a great deal of discussion of the "essential benefits" that had to be included — yadda, yadda, yadda. Still, what it would *cost* the patient to access care was not the subject of much conversation.

Patient costs are last to be considered

These additional out-of-pocket costs can be critical as to whether people are actually able to meet their medical needs and take steps to keep themselves or their family members healthy.

With economic support cushioning the economics of purchasing coverage, and essential benefits offering "free" preventive care, the sticker shock of deductibles and the impact on the physician-patient relationship *comes only when there is illness.*

Those deductibles readily become a medical debt of the patient — and an accounts receivable — increasing the likelihood of bad patient debt for physicians.

According to a Common Wealth Fund report, the percentages of adults who said it was "somewhat" or "very difficult" or "impossible" to afford their health insurance deductible over the past year included:

- 27 percent of adults making more than $45,960 a year
- 49 percent of adults making $22,980 to $45,960 a year

- 64 percent of adults making $11,490 to $22,980 a year
- 58 percent of adults making less than $11,490 a year[12]

That difficulty in affordability is not academic for the physicians in practice. For them, it's a real challenge to their economic survival as well as their ability to provide care for their patients.

With fixed or declining reimbursements from insurance sources and increased operating costs, the physician's dilemma is the conflict between the patient-physician relationship and the patient-physician financial exchange.

The patient-physician relationship gives the doctor more knowledge of the circumstances of the patient than in a usual business transaction. That knowledge of the individual's personal situation creates the tension.

Patients who need increased physician and other medical care and services frequently have economic issues, often created by the illness or as a consequence of illness. These patients frequently can't work or are restricted in their ability to work and require the time and attention of family members. Family income is often impacted as caregiving takes priority over producing income.

The Physician's Dilemma

The physicians' dilemma — given the limited time they have to produce revenue and the fixed reimbursements that impact income — is how to balance the economic needs of the practice with a compassionate response to a patient's situation.

Heart-directed write-offs of patient debts can spell financial failure for the practice. Worse, there's a joker in that deck. If the patient has insurance, this act of charity could also cause the physician to be accused of insurance fraud by a health plan.

This land mine is contained in the small print of the physician's participation agreement with the health plans. Most physician-participation contracts with health plans contain a provision that actually prohibits physicians from waiving the patient's portion of the fee. It states that there is no insurance coverage for services that a patient can receive without cost.

> The land mine is in the small print

Therefore, if a physician waives the patient portion of a bill, an insurance company could claim that the patient is receiving the services without cost and therefore deny the physician the customary reimbursement. (The physician would have to have a financial-hardship policy that documents the patient's financial conditions, obtaining such documentation as patient tax returns to qualify for accommodating a patient's economic hardship — a burden to administer.)

The devil isn't *in* the details; the devil *added* these details.

Other Provisions also Work Against a 'Heart' Approach

If the physician's bill is $100, and the insurance covers 80 percent, should the physician waive the patient portion of 20 percent, the insurance company could argue that the physician's bill was false, as it was really only valued at $80. The plan argues that it is responsible only for 80 percent of what the patient is actually liable for; since 20 percent ($20) was waived. The insurance is applied only to the balance.

As a real-world example, a medical practice insured their employees with HealthNet and (as a courtesy to their employees), waived the patient co-payment. The practice became subject to an inquiry and had to defend itself in a review by HealthNet's Special Investigations Unit.

Yes, insurers will stoop that low.

Employing the External Bill Collector

"Hard core" collections against patients who likely have both medical and money problems are contrary to most physicians' personal values and sentiments. Physicians contribute to the patient's debt load not out of desire but out of economic necessity.

Bankruptcies are an escape hatch from the burdens of medical costs, which can weigh heavily on families. Bankruptcies are not a panacea, as it is like a "Mark of Cain" on a person's record for 10 years, negatively impacting everything from the ability to get a mortgage to even being excluded from a job. Many employers worry (wrongly) that a person who has gone bankrupt will prove to be a less-than-stable and honest worker.

In the period before bankruptcy, there is still a burden. The CDC, The Centers for Disease Control, reported that in 2011 one in five families could not pay their medical obligations. This economic stress negatively impacts their physical health and discourages them from seeking further medical care because of an outstanding bill. As pointed out earlier, this choice further deteriorates the health status of the individual, exacerbating the situation.[13]

Physicians must generate enough income to cover their practice expenses and support their family. When payment from the insurance plan is insufficient due to poor coverage or limitations on that coverage, the patient remains fully responsible. The patient-physician relationship now becomes a financial relationship.

With their heart, physicians would gladly forgive. But with their head, they can neither absorb rising losses at a time of increasing expenses nor risk administrative sanctions (or worse) from the insurance carriers.

The *heart* and the *head* — a struggle seldom experienced by other small businesses.

What would you do, if you were in the doctor's shoes?

Why Change is Needed

Story #3

I saw your news report on my local news and was moved to tears at the generosity and kindness you two gentleman have shown. I am in need of help. Please!

I am a 59 year old widow. Two years ago, this August 8th, my husband of 35 years, the love of my life, committed suicide due to depression. ... Though my everyday existence is filled with heartache, grief and loneliness, it is also a daily struggle financially for me as well. The day [my husband] died, I lost his pension. What life insurance he had covered his funeral expense, his headstone and some outstanding financial obligations.

I am struggling daily and working two jobs, sometimes 14 hours per day, just to make my mortgage payment, utilities and payments on a 12 year old vehicle. In addition, I still have outstanding medical bills for my husband and also myself, which total approximately $4,000.[14]

AGGRAVATING THE WOUND: IT'S NOT JUST THE BILL COLLECTOR

Chapter 4 — Ashton

"The bill collector? He's the guy who sweeps up after the parade."

— ABE "WALKING BEAR" SANCHEZ,
CREDIT INDUSTRY SAVANT

Chances are that almost anyone reading this book has either experienced the burden of medical bills or has close family members or friends who have. As Robert Goff explains, this is true even for people having "comprehensive" insurance coverage. But the person *most* worried about those unpaid bills is the doctor and hospital. Oh, yes, and *their* lenders and creditors.

Robert paints a grim picture. If a doctor works from his or her *heart*, it is at their economic peril. If they work from the heart and not the ledger, there goes their income and the practice along with it. If they solely work from the *head*, this requires that they expend every effort to recover monies owed. When their staff has given up on that effort, the outside bill collector is brought in. It can get ugly.

We All Want Our Money

Popular perception notwithstanding, there is a strong case to be made for having empathy for the bill collector who is called upon to recover errant dollars. Consider his or her position in this matter.

Let's start with the internal collector, who works at the medical practice or hospital, and the external collector, who works for a collection agency or attorney. They share the same purpose but not always the same tools and approaches.

Let's also agree that it's largely a hard, thankless job to chase down monies owed their employer physician, medical group, or hospital. Their work is complicated by inadequate training, outdated technology, and untimely, incorrect, or confusing billing practices. Add to this the physicians themselves, who often have a mixed mind about collecting on monies owed (the *head* vs. *heart* problem).

> Collections is a thankless job

What also needs to be respected is that a medical practice is the small business Robert and I both describe. Unlike businesses that can protect themselves by requiring people to pass credit checks or put down large deposits before goods or services are provided, a medical facility welcomes you (almost) unquestionably if you have insurance, accepts a small co-pay, performs the service, bills you or your insurance, and waits for payment.

And waits. And waits.

The early guardians of the bottom line and the financial health of the practice reside inside the practice's walls. This staff might sport such titles such as "Director of Credit," "Patient Affairs," "Account Manager," or "Customer Service," and the like. In larger, sophisticated operations, they are judged by their "revenue cycle performance" along with their ability to retain patient good will.

Overall, they do a respectable job of getting the money and not ruffling feathers; the doctor's or hospital's reputation will suffer if they are abusive, disrespectful or insensitive.

However, even doing the best that they can, they will fail to collect every last dollar. The causes are myriad: Unresolvable disputes, neglect or spite on the part of the patient, a need to work on current accounts before they get old, doctors who allow their hearts to overrule their heads and allow impossibly low-payment or high-payment plans, and personal financial conditions that make a successful repayment schedule highly unlikely.

The latter is exacerbated by patients being required to pay a larger and larger portion of their healthcare, even with insurance. Owed balances are up 15 percent to 20 percent from 8 percent to 10 percent just a few years back. Deductibles are higher, and co-pays at time of service are following close behind.

This lack of success in bringing in the money can, literally, put a practice into *critical care.* The larger the practice or medical group, the greater the need for positive cash flow. In hospitals, bad debt is called "uncompensated care," and it adds up — some $4.1 billion in 2011, or 5.9 percent of hospital expenses — a rate that has been increasing at 8 percent per year according to a report in *Healthcare Finance News.*[1]

The Affordable Care Act will not prove of help. It's projected that people least able to afford their medical bills will be most likely to select the cheaper Bronze plans available at insurance exchanges, which pay only 60 percent of costs. A steep out-of-pocket maximum of $5,950 for individuals or $11,900 for families awaits the family or individual unlucky enough to need insurance.

This has resulted in medical centers taking the more proactive approach of "previewing" services with prospective patients to determine their ability and attitude toward meeting these obligations, as well as proactively turning collectors into "financial counselors."

Thus, we are back to the challenge of training and technology with the added overhead of staffing.

Even attempting to capture these skills and technologies by outsourcing or by bringing professional collection consultants and collectors in-house is problematic. The Minnesota attorney general's office recently sued Accretive Health for alleged violations of patient privacy and consumer-protection laws because of their aggressive "counseling" of patients in the hospital — literally at bedside, in a few cases.[2]

Once a third-party collector is "embedded" (hmmmm, battle-field term here; the euphemism for their work is "back-office debt collection"), they work intently to extract payments and promises and go so far as to require the patient to hand over a credit card or even make a payment in advance of service.

This is not just problematic. If it crosses a line, it becomes a violation of the FDCPA (Fair Debt Collections Practices Act), which requires a third-party collector to provide a "mini-Miranda" warning in disclosing that they are a debt collector, advising the patient that they intend to collect a debt, and stating that any information obtained will be used for that purpose.

The collector may have violated the FDCPA as well by looking indistinguishable from a hospital employee or otherwise processing your medical information under such guise. Interestingly, if they are actual employees of the hospital, it would appear that doing everything possible to collect a debt is fair game. Always check with state laws to see if the hospital is held to all the same rules applicable to a creditor.

A settlement agreement barred Accretive from operating in the state for at least two years or no more than six. The company, one of the largest in its field, at one point missed a deadline to file restated financials, which triggered a delisting of its stock by the New York Stock Exchange.[3]

If this can happen to presumed "experts" in the field of outsourced collections, what in the world can a community hospital or medical practice hope to do internally? They went into business to be doctors — not bill collectors or relationship-management experts.

Hospital Collections Under Scrutiny

Proposed IRS 501(r) regulations for nonprofit hospitals will require them to allow patients 120 days to resolve a bill before taking "extraordinary collection action" described as "reporting the debt to a credit bureau, filing lawsuits or liens, and garnishing wages." The guideline also mirrors proposed changes to the Fair Debt Collection Practices Act (FDCPA) in a bill introduced in the U.S. House of Representatives and now in effect from December 31, 2014.

A cornerstone of the proposed Medical Debt Responsibility Act will be a requirement that hospitals *and* collection agencies remove paid medical debt from credit reports within 45 days.[4] Given all the costs of meeting these conditions, how can a practice focus on creating dependable and timely cash flow to keep the doors open and the lights on?

The solution for the practice or hospital is always in *people, processes and technology* — all of which need to support their overall theme or mission. Practices that have the right (and well-trained) people in place, well-thought-out policies translated into efficient processes, and the technology to tie all the elements all together will suffer the least.

They need to set in place a comprehensive *policy* supported by a specific *process* in moderating patient payments, *people* trained in that process, and *technology* that facilitates the visit-to-cash process to keep things flowing properly.

Empathy for the bill collector?

Any question about how many medical practices have these elements competently handled? You really don't want to know. Whether you read this book as a patient, doctor, or internal or external bill collector, you need to read it carefully to understand the interplay. Each of the roles, if fashioned to maximize the balance of mutual respect and a clear understanding of economic realities, can contribute to a better overall experience.

Bill collectors probably rank somewhere in social status below the insurance-company executive and somewhat above the beltway politician. Both of them keep the bill collector employed, by the way. The physician is just the middleman who provides a constant flow of unfortunates.

Since neither the debtor nor the bill collector fully appreciates each other's world, much less their assigned role in the larger world of debt, you can understand the tension and distrust. It has been my lifelong purpose to debunk myths and to establish the space for a working respect. This is both needed and appropriate in the process of liberating ourselves from the burden of being a "victim" on one side or a "persecutor" on the other.

Let me address this chapter to the two of you, the collector and the patient, should you ever find yourselves in each other's company. What you learn here could serve to make encounters more respectful, less hostile, and even — if you can imagine it — more productive. You need to both deal with and adapt to a world not of your making.

Goody, Goody — More Debtors!

Attention, agencies and debt buyers: The ACA will undoubtedly increase the number of debtors in the pipeline and on their way to your desk. Those bills will prove harder to collect.

Consider that more than 47 million non-elderly Americans were uninsured in 2012. Decreasing the number of people in this group is a key goal of the ACA, which provides Medicaid or subsidized coverage to qualifying individuals with incomes up to 400 percent of poverty, beginning in 2014.[5]

The majority of the uninsured are in low-income working families. Reflecting the more-limited availability of public coverage, adults are more likely to be uninsured than children. People of color are at higher risk of being uninsured than non-Hispanic Whites. A study published in the *American Journal of Public Health* in 2009 found that lack of health insurance is associated with about 45,000 excess preventable deaths per year.

Through the ACA we can expect fewer preventable deaths per year, but the irony is that we can also can expect more people will return to health — only to have to deal with the debt brought about by the life-saving ministrations. New debtors will be created, and more bill collectors will be required.

Perform a Google search on "medical debt," and see the result: At least 22 million references will pop up. There are links that can transport you to sites that will claim to erase the debt, help you file bankruptcy (because of the debt), teach you to cope with the debt, manage the debt, negotiate the debt, and deal with the debt if you are a senior citizen or a college student — *all this on just the first few pages of Google results!*

The movie industry may (as it always has) give us a glimpse of the future. I mean *waaaay* in the future, in which the collection of medical bills reaches a logical conclusion. Well, at least to the hospital CFO, or the scriptwriter, in this case.

In *Repo Men*, Jude Law and Forrest Whitaker are repossession agents who track down medical debtors. "You didn't pay for that kidney.... I'm here to recover it and bring it back to the good doctor." And out comes the scalpel.[6]

Is this really that far-fetched? Will medical practices have to (not just want to) have some form of "walletectomy" available for use on patients who do not make payment in full?

Medical offices — in particular, clinics — are becoming very creative in meeting this challenge, to the point of helping to secure credit for prospective patients and even counsel them in cases of financial distress. A Houston Law Center research showed:

- Clinics offering credit counseling: 30.4 percent
- Clinics mentioning credit: 48.5 percent
- Clinics mentioning a limited number of credit options: 62.1 percent (of the clinics mentioning credit)
- Clinics marketing themselves *because* of the credit they offer or marketing their credit options: 52 percent (of clinics mentioning credit)

In this scenario, your doctor is indistinguishable from your banker, or the local car dealership. The researcher relates a story told by a sales rep for a major medical lender for fertility clinics, describing how she would coach clinic staff to frame the cost of fertility treatment in monthly payments instead of total cost in order to attract more customers.

It makes sense. Saying, "For just $225 a month, you can have a baby" is a lot more persuasive than saying, "IVF will cost you $16,000." Long after they are toting a baby, they will be "toting the note."

If going through your doctor's or clinic's financing institution is not palatable, why not simply employ a credit card to pay those bills?

That's controversial, as well. In Illinois, a "nonprofit" hospital steered patients to a credit card company called CareCredit to finance its patients' bills that stretched beyond three months.

This card provider offered deferred-interest plans for up to 18 months, and — get this — counseled patients that they could avoid all interest charges if they paid off their debts in the agreed-upon term.

Customers who failed to meet the terms were subject to interest rates of about 23 percent or higher for the entire debt, and the interest rate could rise to 27 percent or higher on delinquent payments, according to their application.[7]

So, no matter how we end up on the gurney, a scalpel will be there to work just as skillfully on our wallet as on our pancreas. That's where bill collecting kicks in.

The External Collector — The Infamous 'Third Party'

Even if the internal bill collectors believe their job is tough, few of them would care to work in a collection agency chasing the medical debt *they* failed to collect. The pressure and the environment is similar to jumping from the frying pan into the fire.

> Collections — a tough, but necessary, job

People within an agency have titles, but not nearly as honorific: "Small Balance Desk" or "Legal" are examples. Whatever their title, these people labor away to bring back hundreds of millions of dollars annually to America's businesses and bankers — and even to our local, state and national governments. Medical debt is not the largest debt out there.

Just how tough — and necessary — is this job that *somebody* has to do? Is bad debt that bad?

Most recent estimates of annual medical bad-debt write-off in America runs in excess of *$100 billion.* Receivables that are aged past 90 days have only a 76 percent chance of ever being paid. The longer a debt is owed, the less likely it is a creditor will be paid. That's why the intensity and volume of collection calls and letter contacts ramp up the older the account becomes.

It used to be that the "Thin Blue Line" identified the meager amount of police *vs.* a staggering amount of bad guys. Today, it's the "Thin Red Line" of collectors, credit managers and collection agencies that stand between millions of non-paying accounts and the solvency of their employers.

In addition to the medical industry, those employing bill collectors are businesses, banks, and state, local and federal governmental agencies (the IRS is slated to add an additional 16,000 collectors this coming year). It would appear that any enterprise not working on a cash basis is chasing debt.

What Do These Overwhelmed Warriors Get for Their Efforts?

Civil lawsuits brought by consumers against debt collectors, purchasers and other credit-reporting agencies increased 52.5 percent in FY 2009, according to the Administrative Office of the U.S. Courts. In the year ending September 30, 2009, exactly 6,463 civil cases were filed for redress under consumer credit statutes — the

Fair Credit Reporting Act (FCRA) and the Fair Debt Collections Practices Act (FDCPA). This compares to 4,239 cases in 2008 and 1,192 cases in FY 2005.

More recent figures show that the desire — need — to sue third-party collectors is not abating.[8] So, whether a creditor, a debtor or a collector, the world is a much more complicated place than imagined. It's not easy for any of the parties, and the rules always seem to be changing.

Are we tired of this yet? Are you getting the sense that *it's the system that needs to be changed?*

Why Change is Needed

Story #4

To Whom It May Concern, I watched you on channel 11 last night. What you are doing is wonderful.

There are people out there, like my mom, who has practically nothing, and has medical bills. Last year my mom fell and broke her hip. I thought we were finished with the bills that came, but last week she received 2 bills from the ambulance company for about $500. I called them and told them she's got nothing left and lives on $1200 a month social security. The woman told me there is nothing they can do. She's got to pay the 2 bills.

She has a hard time living on $1200 a month. I'm an only child, and try to help her as much as I can. But *it's hard when everything falls on me. I tried to fix this (hospital) problem and got the run around. No one ... would help me.*

The social worker at the hospital told me she had a friend that helps people fix their medical insurance problems like this one. When I called her, she was very nice. I thought she was going to help me. I asked her if there was a charge for her help, and she told me she would charge me $2,500. I almost fell over. I explained to her that I didn't have that kind of money and hung up.

I'm hoping you can help us with these ambulance bills. I look forward to hearing from you.[9]

OBAMACARE AND NATIONAL HEALTH REFORM: A FAULTY VISION — BUT NOT FOR THE REASONS YOU THINK

Chapter 5 — Goff

The concept is simple. Get 100 percent of the U.S. population insured.

With 100 percent insured, every citizen would have coverage, forever removing economics as a barrier to obtaining healthcare services. All of us would have coverage, protecting ourselves and our families from economic devastation if medical services are needed but out of financial reach. Wisely, the cost of delivering care would be spread over the entire population, in effect nationalizing the cost of medical care but not the organization of care delivery.

No more pre-existing condition exclusions. No more lifetime caps of medical coverage. No more insurance available only through one's employer (itself a vestige of World War II price controls).

Healthcare providers, hospitals, doctors, and others would no longer carry the burden of providing services without payment — uncompensated care — having to pass those costs on to others, or increasing the costs for those who are insured by reducing the cost of care for the uninsured.

Don't force people into one plan; give them *choice,* and allow people to make their own decision from among comparable plans. That way, people can readily choose the plan they prefer based on price, the carrier's reputation, and its included providers, hospitals and physicians.

Keep confusion out of the selection of plans by mandating that each plan offer the same benefit package, labeled Bronze, Silver, Gold, and Platinum.

For those of low economic means, expand Medicaid coverage. Bring Medicaid insurance to those with incomes up to 132 percent of the Federal Poverty Level. For those of more modest means, subsidize the purchase of approved insurance for those between 133 percent and 400 percent of the Federal Poverty Level.

Finally, impose consequences for those who try to avoid purchasing or obtaining coverage.

Great concept, that. Universal health insurance, universal health coverage. No one need fear the cost of illness, and no provider need fear a loss on providing care. Allow the healthcare delivery system to remain in private hands, and let insurance companies offer their policies for everyone.

Health Reform, the Affordable Care Act, which created what is proudly or derisively called "Obamacare," largely changed health insurance, dramatically providing access, while minimally, if at all, changing the structure of health care delivery.

Universal health insurance, not a universal healthcare system

In the process, ACA created some real devils in the details.

Access? Access to What?

"If you like your doctor, you can keep your doctor."

This was an unfortunately worded political promise, which did not include an asterisk to qualify it — because your ability to keep your doctor, well, kind of depends. It depends on whether or not your physician chose, or was chosen, to participate in a product that is approved under the ACA.

Health reform — Obamacare — provides for access to health insurance coverage for those not able to obtain coverage through their employer: For the poor and working poor, expanded Medicaid coverage; for the working middle class, more traditional, commercially offered health plans with income subsidies for premiums if needed.

However, there is no provision to increase physician participation or protections to assure that physicians currently being used could continue to be used.

Expanding Medicaid does not mean that participation in Medicaid by medical providers magically will increase because of Health Reform. The increasing number of people now obtaining coverage through Medicaid will likely begin to have a problem in finding participating physicians or other providers that are accepting new patients.

Obtaining care may become difficult, even through traditional providers to this population group — the very fine community health centers or the more the notorious Medicaid-mills, or even the hospital emergency room. Care will be a problem in the absence of increased physician participation.

Increasing physician participation would require increasing compensation for physician services, which have long been so woefully underfunded that physicians stopped accepting Medicaid beneficiaries.

Physicians largely did not want to abandon this segment of their communities' populations; they have been forced out of them because of low reimbursement rates.

Physicians, even with the low reimbursement rates, were often willing to accept in their practice a percentage of people who were Medicaid patients in their communities, but Medicaid rules required physicians accepting Medicaid to be open to *all* new Medicaid patients. Those rules prohibit limiting the number of Medicaid patients in the practice without closing their entire patient panel to all Medicaid patients.

Even the most willing physicians could not financially afford to have too large a percentage of Medicaid patients (with low reimbursements consuming limited appointment time) who drive out higher-pay sources — not if they wanted to maintain a practice.

The only option for survival for some is to refuse to see any and all Medicaid patients — or to become a high-volume Medicaid "clinic," which have earned a reputation for volume of patients seen over quality of care delivered.

The out-of-network trap

On the commercial side, those choosing to purchase approved coverage and take advantage of the economic subsidies had to purchase from a limited number of offerings on the Health Insurance Exchange.

These approved products all had to meet Federal requirements for the benefits included, and to ease comparability, had to be standardized to levels called Bronze, Silver, Gold, and Platinum — each level offering proportionately exactly the same coverage, regardless of the insurance carrier offering the plans.

The difference comes down to premium price and network: The medical community contracted to provide coverage care under the policies. Here, the differentials can be dramatic.

To a great extent, products offered through a Health Insurance Exchange do not provide coverage for out-of-network care, *except in an emergency*. Indeed, of the 64 products offered on the NYS Health Insurance Exchange, in the New York City market, *not one* offered a product or availability of coverage for out-of-network services.

Any and all care, to have insurance coverage, must be provided within the approved contracted network of providers, physicians, hospitals, and other healthcare providers. This has given rise to the derisive description, "Narrow Networks" — or some would say, "Claustrophobic Networks."

The choice of who is in the network is made by the insurance carrier. How that decision is made by the carrier is largely a black box, without transparency and without regard to any existing patient-physician relationships.

> Not just narrow networks — claustrophobic networks

Insurance carriers, using proprietary data, proprietary algorithms, without accountability to any person or agency, chose its Narrow Network and chose the physicians and hospitals that would be included for coverage. The physicians chosen, as well as those excluded, were never provided with any data or appeal rights. If excluded, they were denied even the opportunity to apply for inclusion.

For example, Empire Blue Cross Blue Shield created its Narrow Network, called "Pathways," by excluding every academic medical center in New York City and all the physicians that were associated with those institutions during its 2014 offering.

It appears that insurance carriers excluded and included providers based on unit price of services — that is, how much they had been paying the providers *under their existing contracts.* Quality and efficiency were neither measured nor considered. Health-insurance companies, which had long supported the concept of the "Patient Centered Medical Home," which recognizes quality and access in the delivery of primary care, abandoned many a physician who had earned the designation of being a Patient Centered Medical Home outside of these Narrow Networks.

In other words, you can keep your own physician if that physician is in your insurance company's approved network and is compelled to take low rates regardless of how this will impact the quality in the care delivered.

Hospital participation was also included or excluded based on unit price. Major teaching institutions, including those that are specialty focused, such as NYC's Sloan-Kettering Cancer Center, were often left out. In New Hampshire, where only one company is offering products on that state's Health Exchange. Anthem, a Blue Cross/Blue Shield Affiliated company, excluded 10 of the 26 hospitals in the state.

These Narrow Networks are also most often state specific, meaning that, for an area like the Tri-state area — the New York, New Jersey, Connecticut region — where crossing borders for care is as common as crossing them for shopping, you can't cross the state lines for covered care, even if your insurance company sells the product in each of the states.

Your coverage ends at the border, unless you are lucky enough to have access to cross-state coverage and purchase it. This is one of those details often not discovered until care is needed, or even after it is obtained, substantially increasing the patient's economic risk.

Who are the "chosen" ones, and by what rules?

This is very problematic for patients living near the borders of states, where often the nearest medical providers are across a state line.

The problem of the Narrow Network and access to your physician took on added complexity and confusion because many insurance companies chose to eliminate some specific existing products or even eliminate entire product lines, such as individual and small-group polices that were being sold off the Health Insurance Exchange.

People who had such coverage, finding their policies being canceled, were provided "replacement" policies, but that replacement was based on the health plan's Narrow Network, disrupting long-standing physician/patient relationships. Public "disclosure" that the physician and hospital network had changed was less than prominent.

Just who is in these "chosen" networks has been a source of confusion and mystery to patients and physicians alike. Health Plans do not make it easy, with a wide array of network and product names constantly being added while implementing new rules for the participating physician.

United has a series of products called "Core," "Metro" and "Charter." Physicians that are participating in their networks, called "Freedom" and "Liberty," are not participating in these products, unless the patient is in a hospital and then the physician is participating. How is a physician or a patient to keep this nuance clear? What is the likelihood that the patient will be caught in the confusion?

From the aspect of clinical care, there's little support in the health plans for continuity in care, even though continuity is considered an important element in the quality of care.

Verifying that your physicians are participating in one of these "chosen" networks is a challenge in itself. Recent reviews of the online directories by the health plans have revealed high degrees of inaccuracies as well as the lack of availability of the listed physicians willing to accept new patients.

In California, 12.8 percent of the physicians listed in the Anthem Health online directory were found not to be accepting new patients; they could not keep even the office locations accurate for 25 percent of the physicians listed.[1]

"If you like your current health insurance plan, you can keep it" is the other oft-repeated political statement that should have come with an asterisk. Yes, you can keep it, *if* it meets the federal requirements.

The ACA established a set of essential benefits which all health insurance plans must cover. If your current health insurance plan did not include all of the *essential* benefits, it could no longer be sold after a transition period. (Under political pressure, states could extend the life of these non-conforming plans for an additional year — a state-by-state decision.)

Non-conforming policies under Health Reform took on the label of "junk policies" because they often have large gaps in the health benefits or those benefits are accessible only after a deductible so high that they provide only catastrophic benefits.

Some People Want Junk

However, junk policies did satisfy the needs and desires of some purchasers. The non-conforming policies were referred to as "limited-benefit" or "mini-meds," and they appealed to people purchasing individual policies. Some argue that the limits of these plans allowed people the freedom to purchase coverage that met their needs and a level of affordability that was greater than that now demanded of them by conforming products.

For example, for a single male purchasing a mini-med policy that excluded maternity benefits, as 66 percent of such policies did, the sacrifice for cost savings was not a hard decision.[2]

However, the purchasers of such policies on price alone learned of the limitations when they needed more than what was allowed. This "surprise" created major economic burdens for them and medical debt for their caregivers.

In fairness to the legislation and the amount of junk policies being sold, it was not a bad idea to require minimum standards for what must be covered under a health insurance policy. These requirements were implemented for all health insurance that sold on and off the Health Insurance Exchange.

Essential health benefits that must be included in all policies are:

- Ambulatory patient services; emergency services
- Hospitalization
- Maternity and newborn care
- Mental health and substance-use-disorder services, including behavioral health treatment
- Prescription drugs; rehabilitative services and devices
- Preventive and wellness services along with chronic-disease management
- Pediatric services, including oral and vision care

Within these categories are definitions of coverage that have given rise to the controversial requirement to provide coverage for birth control.

To the extent that there continues to be no national consensus about universal access to birth control and no state-sanctioned religion to guide such decisions, the benefit requirements are seen by some as a tool of social engineering or a device to install by fiat one view of the reproductive-rights debate.

In retrospect, it would have been wiser to exclude a mandate on birth-control coverage and to provide for its purchase on an individual basis by a simple rider outside of the employer-required benefit package. Of course, in mandating a set of benefits as a minimum, there are those who find such benefits to be more than they desire, or need, e.g., the bachelor male and pre-natal care.

Political Statements Require Asterisks

"Your health insurance costs will not go up" is another oft-heard political statement that should have come with an asterisk.

For those with policies that exclude some of the above, the cost of the replacement policies would, of necessity, increase. For example, junk insurance policies often had exclusions such as no coverage for mental health or substance-abuse treatment, limits on pharmacy benefits to generics only, or excluded maternity, or polices that offered a lifetime cap of $1 million on payouts. In the thinking of some, the $1 million limit will never be reached, and valuable dollars are saved in premium costs.

> When "cheap" gets expensive

This is when cheap gets expensive, as cancer, organ transplants and premature births all have lifelong higher costs. That cap is breached to the detriment of the policyholder, but the limits of that cap are not appreciated until the service is needed.

The fact is, increases in benefits are not appreciated by those who have to pay a higher premium for services that they do not expect to use. Any presumed savings on premiums is regretted when superior coverage is needed.

More than half of the personal bankruptcies in this nation currently relate to medical bills and the economic stress that is placed on families and individuals by the cost of care. The ACA was designed to address this tragedy, but does it?

Bronze, Silver, Gold, and Platinum

The four categories of coverage are not necessarily protection from medical debt and family financial destruction (see charts on pages 8 and 9).

> Not all that glitters is good

Bronze, the plan with the most affordable premium, is actuarially designed to provide coverage for only 60 percent of the costs of covered medical care. That leaves 40 percent as the financial responsibility of the patient and family. The deductibles are at $3000 for an individual and $6000 for a family.

The out-of-pocket cap is at $6,350 for the individual and $12,700 for the family. For Gold, the actuarial design is 70 percent of the costs covered with $2,000 individual deductible and $4,000 family deductible, with $5,500 out-of-pocket maximum for the individual and $11,000 for the family.

Clearly, there are those of modest means for whom such risk can expose them to personal or family economic devastation.

For the healthcare provider, physicians, and hospitals, medical debt will remain an issue and a problem. Patient financial responsibilities are not eliminated by the ACA and the public may be lulled into a false sense of security that they are. Under three of the four benefit plans, Bronze, Silver, and Gold, deductibles remain; and co-insurance — the portion that a patient must pay toward each service — also remains.

Patient financial responsibilities are an economic risk to the healthcare provider, as well. The physician still has to implement payment policies to assure that the cost of the services they provide are paid, and they take the risk that the services provided will not be paid, largely by the patient.

For healthcare providers, there is an added "risk," that of ineligibility after the fact.

A patient's eligibility is not guaranteed. Even if a provider verifies coverage at time of care, those individuals who purchase their coverage on the Exchange are given a grace period to pay their monthly insurance premium. That is, the provider will receive a confirmation that the patient is covered even if the premium remains unpaid, up to 90 days after it was due.

While insurance carriers are required to pay claims during the first 30 days, they are, with full knowledge, misrepresenting eligibility for the next 60 days.

The healthcare provider is obligated to provide care during that 60-day period and is at risk if the policy is terminated because the premium was not paid, adding injury to the insult, as the risk goes back 60 days. The health plan is liable for just 30 days of claims in this 90-day grace period.

This translates to risk exposure to the providers of care and the potential for increasing their bad debt as well as the medical-debt load of their patients.

Health Reform is Really Insurance Reform

Let me repeat. Health Reform is really insurance reform.

The ACA addressed major barriers to purchasing health insurance, the elimination of pre-existing conditions, providing coverage for children up to age 26 under a family policy, making coverage available to individuals, not employer-dependent, and providing expanded Medicaid. All this, along with premium subsidies, to increase affordability for a large segment of the middle class.

The ACA did little to change the fundamental structure of care delivery. It does not move hospitals to areas where they are needed, increase the supply of primary-care physicians, increase ambulatory-care options, or close duplicative or unnecessary hospitals.

All of the needed re-engineering of the care delivery structure has been left to the healthcare industry, which has proven to be more dedicated to the protection of the status quo and their bottom line than reforming itself by meeting evolving community medical needs.

Health Reform is trying to motivate the re-engineering through Medicare, the health insurance plan for those 65 years of age and older, via the creation of Accountable Care Organizations, ACOs.

"Re-engineering" serves the status quo

ACOs are organizations of healthcare providers formed for the purpose of contracting with Medicare to provide services to Medicare beneficiaries with economic- and quality-performance measures for which they will be accountable. The providers in an ACO are responsible to deliver and arrange care, with economic benefits if successful.

However, to be successful, most ACOs try to create their own Narrow Network (as in, try to limit their referral networks to garner control and reduce costs) to provide for care to Medicare patients. The structure of financial and quality measures are such that an ACO will attempt to keep all care in its network. While Medicare beneficiaries are not penalized if they obtain care outside of an ACO's network, the emphasis on providers of care within the network aim to keep patients in the network.

What may be best for the patient may be secondary to the organization's goals.

Shades of an HMO.

The ACOs, to date, have had mixed performance in delivering on these twin goals, quality and costs. Yes, they focus a community of physicians on goals of cost and quality, but in the process, they have to develop another administrative structure that consumes dollars which might otherwise go into patient care.[3]

Commercial payers have looked at the ACO program of Medicare and asked, "How I can get in on it?" This is better translated as, "How can I put physicians and other healthcare providers at economic risk for the cost of the care they provide and transfer all or part of that economic risk from me, the insurer?"

The result is the development of shared savings and accountable care payment models by commercial payers seeking to emulate the Medicare ACO, even though the results have been mixed.

As yet, there is no discussion of the fundamental structure of care delivery, a structure that's the source for the high costs of health care: A surplus of high-cost hospital facilities and a shortage of lower-cost alternatives in ambulatory and home care.

Houston, we have a (systemic) problem!

Why Change is Needed

Story #5

Amount Owed — Approximately $1000.00

If some/all of this debt were paid, It would be a tremendous burden off my shoulders. I would have my life back. I would be able to rest. This debt causes me tremendous stress, & a feeling of hopelessness, it's the last thing I think of when I go to bed & the first thing I think of when I wake up. My credit rating went from Satisfactory to very poor.[4]

THE BILL COLLECTOR AND THE PATIENT: KNOW AND RESPECT THINE ADVERSARY

Chapter 6 — Ashton

Could there be anyone less esteemed in this world than the bill collector? However, seen through a collector's eyes, could there be any person less honorable than a debtor? Could both be, somehow, very wrong? Could they ever see each other differently?

Stop Calling Me 'Debtor'

Early in the Great Recession, on behalf of those who suddenly found their financial world turned upside down, I wrote and published the following piece as "A Debtor Open Letter" to my associates in the collections industry in an online forum at *Accounts Receivable Management News* (www.InsideARM.com). I have updated it for this book, but I believe the sentiments are just as true now as they were when it was first written.

The Debtor Addresses The Bill Collector.

You may not have noticed it, but bill collectors are getting some pretty bad press recently. Much of it, not just some of it, is well deserved and brought on by your own foibles and how you interact with people like me.

Yes, me. Your target, your bread and butter — the "debtor" — someone with whom you are quite familiar.

I'm the one you keep contacting (if you are heeding collection laws) between the hours of 8:00 a.m. and 9:00 p.m. The one who listens to the voicemails you leave importuning me to call you back about "an important matter." The one you are sending those automated "dunning" letters. The one you sometimes refer to among yourselves as "the deadbeat" or "slug" or worse.

Well, I am tired of being regarded in this fashion and I formally request that you no longer label me a "debtor." I am a fellow citizen. You can start with that, if you feel you have to label me.

I am a father, a husband, a wife, a mother, a grandparent, a student. It happens that I owe money, that I am *waaaay* past due in my payments, and if I am fortunate enough to have a job, I am stretched from payday to payday, just meeting my basic needs.

Once I was called a customer, or a patient, or a client — a "valued" one, at that. Somehow, along the way, I came to be seen as a "consumer" and didn't quite command the same level of respect. As the recession set in deeper, I became a "past due" and then a "problem account."

At the end of this dis-assembly line of my respectability, *you* people showed up. I officially became a *debtor.* That is quite a useful title for you to label me. No one would treat a customer in the way you treat a "debtor." *These* people are accorded an approach more in keeping with their reduced social status.

I don't envy you your job, I want you to know. I respect those among you who are chasing down legitimate debt and doing so in a respectful manner.

There is a subset in that latter group, however, for whom I have no respect — the bottom feeders who buy and pursue debt "out of statute" or with no credible backup but take advantage of the unsophisticated debtor certain to succumb to your near-extortionate techniques. Especially, those accounts you purchase for just pennies on the dollar but pursue for the full amount.

Your industry over time has proven that, because of my ignorance, fear or the time and money required, I will not show up to dispute the lawsuits with which you clog the court system. You have been known to falsify papers, "robo-sign" complaints by the thousands, and then report me to credit bureaus to further drive a stake into my financial heart.[1]

But then, what would you know about *heart?* We understand that, for you and those who bankroll you, this is "just business." Agencies and debt purchasers have very little interest in anything other than profiting off an original creditor's loss and to claw back as many dollars as possible.

You are a big business. You range in sophistication from fly-by-night opportunists to expensive suits catering to wall-street-backed investors. Whatever your credentials, you scurry from debt crevasse to debt crevasse to search out and prey on the vulnerable.

One of your brethren, Arrow Financial Services, which was at one time the country's largest debt buyer, was acquired by Sallie Mae in 2004 — *making this student lender the nation's largest collection agency of that time!*

What shrewd planning on your part! While loading up our children with school debt to support the exploitive for-profit educational industry, you also beefed up your collections operation to handle the delinquencies that you knew would occur. Making money "coming and going," as they say.

Even as Arrow Financial disappeared into the maw of Sallie Mae, collection agency LVNV picked up the scraps, and the process repeated itself.[2]

Companies like these, in collusion with the bankers, Wall-Streeters, and complicit government agencies, have turned my beautiful country into a debtor nation of major proportions.

If your industry had its way, you would bring that Middle Ages institution — debtors prison — back into existence. In fact, you have already done so.

The Minnesota newspaper, *Star Tribune*, reported on a video interview, "Debtor Prison Returns to the US," in which reporter Glenn Howatt discovered that "Creditors are becoming more aggressive about old debt. When they [the debtors] ignore a court judgment, the [bill collector] has a right to get a warrant for your arrest."[3]

He described one woman, arrested over a $250 JC Penney credit card bill, who was processed through the jail system — complete with having to don an orange jail suit — after being hauled in by a sheriff's deputy.

"They manipulated the policeman into being their enforcer," the unhappy debtor complained.

"That's not supposed to be their job.... [The police] have more important things to do," she lamented. However, it's all legal, all by the book, and all at the taxpayer's expense, not borne by the debt collector.

Would JC Penney have, on its own, put this customer in jail? Rather doubtful, and for many good public relations reasons — and beyond. Instead, their decision, like so many other creditors, was to sell off this debt and then turn a blind eye on the purchaser's debt collection techniques and approaches.

Bill Collector: Show Some Backbone

You could refuse to pick up the phone when you can clearly see the debt you are pursuing is questionable at best — and criminal at worst. Surely, you must operate by some code of ethics.

I know that there are those among you who have become heroes to debtors. One such person is a woman who famously turned to

YouTube to let the world know why she had just been "released" from her job as a collector for the Bank of America.[4]

Working as a Customer Service Representative (the corporate code word for "Bill Collector") for a brief stint in 2009, she was a top performer in her department until she began to feel that "there was something inherently evil in my job."

"I'll never forget one cardholder," she relates. This was a 24-year-old single mother who had just lost her own mom and her husband (both in the same year) *and* had learned that she had cancer.

"She told me she couldn't afford the 29.99 percent interest she was being charged or the late fees of $35 each time she was late or paid less than the amount due. I couldn't put her on our (debt relief) program because she did not have enough income. It wasn't up to the Bank of America to help her figure out how get out of debt."

Much to this young lady's credit, she quit that job, saying, "At the end of the day, I did the right thing, and I am sure that God will bless me."

She went on to relate further horror stories, but as a bill collector reading this, you really don't want to hear stories. You only want to hear when you can expect "the check in the mail."

The bottom line is this, Mr. or Ms. Bill Collector: I want respect. If you continue to call me a Debtor, I will surely continue to call you a B***d. This is getting neither of us anywhere. Care to renegotiate the relationship?

And Don't Call Me 'Bill Collector'

On balance, I felt it was only fair to follow that piece by publishing my fictional bill collector's response to the debtor.

* * * * *

This is an open letter to my fellow Americans who are deeply in debt and are now in my world — that of the person who is paid to chase down debt.

I know that people in my industry have been getting some pretty bad press. I will grant that all too many players in the credit, collection and debt purchasing industries deserve condemnation. Just don't put *me* in that box!

I, also, am a fellow citizen.

I am a father, a husband, a wife, a mother, a grandparent, a student. It happens that I earn my living by recovering monies owed by people who have not paid their bills — monies that can make the difference between surviving and failing for the business which has been driven to employ me.

You may not know it, or believe it, but I am important not only to you but also to the economy of this country that we both love so much. I am not your enemy; I am your solution.

There isn't a paycheck that you cash that doesn't come from the successful recovery of outstanding receivables — whether done by hardworking people who manage what we call the "order-to-cash" process within their firm, or the famous "third-party intervention" called collection agencies.

We do more than just collect on accounts, and we are more than mere functionaries or, as you would see us, mercenaries. Those checks that arrive daily at your offices from your customers? Legally, they are little better than promissory notes. Should they "bounce," guess who is called in to save the day?

Are you aware of the times that collectors have coached people away from committing suicide? Are you aware of volunteer pools of collectors who stayed late to make evening calls — not to collect money but to keep elderly people company? Filling the collection plates at church to help the poor? The hours of volunteer service at homeless shelters? Are you aware of the almost industry-wide support we have given to our country's wounded warriors?[5]

Of course not — that wouldn't jibe with your stereotype of what the "heartless bill collector" is all about.

Where you and I can agree is that I have a difficult job. There are fewer of us than there are of you, and the amount of debt out there is staggering.

It's not just a problem here in the US. In one recent year alone, European companies reported write-offs of 300 *billion* Euros. This is an amount equivalent to the entire national debt of Greece!

Considering that last year's write-offs in the U.S. came to more than 2/3 of that number, we have nothing to crow about at home. It's my job as an "accounts receivable recovery specialist" to bring in those dollars.

One in Three Americans is in Collections

According to a report released by the Urban Institute, at least 35 percent of adult Americans have a debt in collections.[6]

Caroline Ratcliffe, a senior fellow at the Urban Institute, related that collections debt "is pervasive and threads through nearly all communities." She added, "Delinquent debt can harm credit scores, which can tip employers' hiring decisions, restrict access to mortgages, and even increase insurance costs."

Just about *everyone* employs bill collectors.

Consider the problems that our governments face — whether it be dollars due our local city hall for sewage fees or parking tickets, or to the U.S. Government for the amazing amount of services for which it charges (such as airport fees, taxes, roads, waterways, and so on). If those bills aren't paid, the service must stop, facilities must close, employees must be sent packing.

All the while, third parties are chasing after these dollars, we are under strict rules by way of the FDCPA (Federal Debt Collections Practices Act) to essentially "be nice" in the course of pursuing consumer debt. Our critics even grow poetic about this.

Back in 2009, this appeared on www.WallStreetPoet.com

Pity the poor bill collector
He loved to call and snarl and hector
To pester 'bout an unpaid debt
'Bout payments that you haven't met.

Pity the poor bill collector
He loved to diddle and dissect ya
Get you feeling beat and small
Just to get you in his thrall.

Pity the poor bill collector
The long-time ego vivisector
Alas these days to get his slice
The poor man finds he must make nice.

Yep, we have to be "nice," as substantial legal protections are in place when consumers deal with third-party collectors. Written into law in 1978, the FDCPA provides a host of restrictions ranging from dealing with acceptable hours of calling, the wording on our dunning letters, and even telephone etiquette.

Sometimes that's me on the phone taking abuse from *you*, making this tough job even more difficult. Collecting money is not easy and not a lot of fun, regardless of how hard we work or diplomatic we are.

You, with your spending and payment habits, are the reason we exist. You could have thought twice about taking on that big-screen

TV, or the trip to the Bahamas or that new car. You might have paid your creditor more promptly. If you had picked up the phone to call them when you found yourself running behind, you would have had an easier time arranging payment terms. Our services would not have been needed.

All too often, you ignored *their* calls. How do we know? Our clients provide us with phone and contact records, documenting their failed attempts.

It is because *you* did not keep your financial agreements that third-party debt-collection agencies are brought into the picture.

I'll grant you, medical debt is the toughest work that we do. We have our own experience of relatives, friends and associates who have been casualties in this never-ending and ongoing tragedy. It is not usual for *us* to be on the receiving end of doctors' collection calls — or their agencies.

So, let me give you some clues about how to work with me once I make contact.

First, be sure that I am calling about *your* debt and not someone else's. Believe it or not, a lot of people share your name and your city, and I am no more interested in wasting my time than you are in wasting ours. Verify account numbers, dates of debt, even your correct name, its spelling, and your proper address.

Be civil. Don't curse me or tell me where to get off. I don't expect you to be thrilled that I am on the phone with you, but I do expect you to give me the same respect you feel that you deserve.

If we do manage to get to the stage of working out a payment program, don't set one up with me that you will not be able to keep. "Broken promises" are the trigger in our industry for escalating our efforts and rolling out the big guns. Better to have me go back to the original creditor with a credible sob story and a suggestion for less-than-optimal payment agreement than with a request for suit.

Do *not* provide me with your bank account and routing numbers. That advice goes counter to what is in my industry's best interests — but as a between-you-and-me thing, this is a suggestion that you will be glad you followed. Don't make it easy for the collector to get a summons and attach your account.

Now, here's a tip on how to deal with over-aggressive collection agencies chasing down your medical debt. Ask for a "fee breakdown," as you believe that there may be billing errors. It can be almost impossible for the agency to provide such details without violating the Health Insurance Portability and Accountability Act (HIPAA). Dispute the bill, and always within 30 days of receiving the first collection letter, and let the collector twist in the wind! (Can't believe I shared this information — but you did want me to be more empathetic to your situation, right?)[7]

Lastly, you have every right to terminate a conversation if it is not going in the right direction and to request that all communications must henceforth be by written correspondence. Oh, and verbally direct me never to call you at your place of work. Be sure to note my name and that conversation on your calendar — you will need those details when you show up in court to sue me for "harassment."

In the meantime, Mr. or Ms. Person-Who-Owes, let's do our best to work with each other to get your finances back on track and your creditor happy. Work with me; I am here to help —and, the more engaged I am, the more likely a resolution will be found.

* * * * *

Got It. I Understand Both Sides. Now What?

As the debtor, you are not without leverage or resources. Whatever you do, you had better have the facts on your side. Highly edited, below is my best take on some excellent pointers, provided by the Allegheny County Bar Association.

- **Review your bill** immediately upon receipt, for memories get foggy. Confirm that all charges are correct, by letter or phone. If you have a dispute, have them send you their formal dispute-process document. Do *not* make payments until you have covered these steps.
- **Negotiate**. It doesn't hurt to ask for a reduction in fees. You don't get what you don't ask for.
- **Payment plans**. Commit to nothing that your circumstances will not be able to afford. Broken agreements are the first step out the door for most medical collectors. Have it in writing. Negotiate for low or no interest. Agree to pay only for the parts of the bill that are not in dispute.

- **Creditors.** Ooops — they've already employed a third party. Call your provider, and ask them to have the account returned to them by the agency. This is like pulling a bone away from a dog, but if the agency hasn't expended too much effort or wants to keep the client's good will, they will do that. Then, negotiate in earnest with your physician.
- **Be firm with the agency collector.** Ask for proof of the bill in writing. If you have a dispute with the bill, the agency must be notified of this within 30 days of the date of the collection letter, or it will be considered uncontested.[8]

If you really want to know your rights and better use the tools and responses, such as those covered earlier, seek out and buy the *Debt Resisters' Operation Manual,* published by Strike Debt. Caution: You just may turn a bit radical when you finish working through 200+ pages of diatribes and complaints about debt inequities in our economic system.[9]

On the other hand, this may be just the resource needed in your case.[10]

A Serious Road-Bump — Your Credit Report

However gruesome it may be to deal with exorbitant medical bills, billing mistakes that never seem to get resolved, and the bill collectors that just won't go away, those agencies can have a major impact on your credit report, which can linger for years.

Do you realize that some collection agencies or providers using service bureaus, once they realize that their dunning efforts have failed, will submit your name and account to national credit-reporting bureaus? Even a $15 co-pay can sink your credit score. This medical debt showing on your Experian or TransUnion report may prevent you from buying that home, getting that job, or renting that apartment.

Horrible.

But, there is a lot of positive action being taken on this front which will provide you some (future) hope.

According to a recent article in NerdWallet, analytics industry giant FICO (NYSE: FICO) has set about to reform its present credit-reporting system to differentiate medical from non-medical collection agency accounts.[11] As FICO's site declares:

"This will help ensure that medical collections have a lower impact on the score, commensurate with the credit risk they represent. These enhancements lead to a more predictive score. The median FICO Score for consumers whose only major negative references are medical collections will increase by 25 points."[12]

This will not come about overnight, as their "FICO Score 9" product first has to be adopted by the three credit bureaus. As NerdWallet points out, "FICO 9" will give less weight to medical debt, but it will not complexly eliminate the effects of that debt on your credit score. On a bright note, FICO 9 will also disregard medical accounts in collections that were ultimately paid off or settled — as much as half of all medical accounts listed on credit reports.

Your best defense here is to read up on how to get medical — and other — accounts off of your credit report and then act early. Again, NerdWallet to the rescue:

> As of August 2014, the credit scoring model most lenders rely on treats paid and unpaid collections accounts the same. This means that even if you pay the bill, your score likely won't improve as a result (although it will get the bill collector off your back). The best thing to do in this case is to be patient and continue good credit habits, like paying your other bills on time and keeping your credit-card balances low. This will help your credit score bounce back over time.[13]

Consumers, and afflicted patients especially, will have NY State Attorney General Eric Schneiderman to thank for the most recent headlines in the *Wall Street Journal*, "Credit-Reporting Giants Agree to Overhaul."[14]

Although the changes will take up to 40 months to kick in, Equifax, Experian and TransUnion signed an agreement signed to be more proactive in handling complaints about information contained in their credit reports. Until now, consumers had little hope of the agencies actually researching the correctness of creditor-provided data — no better than 15 accounts out of 100, on average. If creditors said the info was "good," *they* had the final say.

Under the new agreement, medical debt (50+ percent of all debt reported) will be treated differently on credit reports. Credit-reporting firms will have to wait 180 days before adding any medical debt information — a grace period that will let patients/consumers clear up discrepancies and catch up with their bills.

Further, medical debt paid by insurance companies will have to be expunged from the report as soon as that happens instead of staying on credit reports up to seven years.

On the other hand, if a bill that you or your insurer paid went into collections by mistake, there are steps you can take to have it removed from your credit report:

- **Gather documentation** — Collect as much documentation as you can that the bill was paid. Ask for payment records from your doctor's office, find copies of canceled checks, or dig up old credit-card statements. Make copies of these documents and include them with your dispute letter.
- **Send written notice** — Alert the credit bureaus that you're disputing the collections. Send a letter to the bureaus reporting the error that explains the nature of the error. (Make sure to check all three of your credit reports to figure out which ones received the wrong information.) Be sure to include documentation of your claim.
- **Keep communicating** — The Fair Credit Reporting Act requires the credit bureaus to follow up on all credit-reporting-error disputes. Keep communicating with the bureaus to

check on the status of your claim, and be prepared to provide additional documentation if requested.

There's no guarantee the error will be removed from your credit report, especially if you have spotty documentation and the doctor's office isn't on your side. Since a poor credit score can make borrowing money really expensive, it's definitely worth a shot.

And you thought your hip transplant or your sextuple-bypass operation was painful!

Why Change is Needed

Story #6

Not sure of the amount but it is extremely high. I'm a young man who is in great shape. I work out every day. Unfortunately I am a Type 1 diabetic who is now suffering from renal failure. I started dialysis and am waiting on a kidney and pancreas transplant. I do not let this hold me down!

But when I receive my new lease on life I would like to be able to start with a clean slate on all levels and the debt is insurmountable! At this point I can't even answer my phone. I just feel when this ordeal is over I would be helped to start anew with this program! I appreciate the time and will be sharing your program via social media and will do my best to spread the word and give back as well. Thank you![15]

OBAMACARE AND THE INSURANCE INDUSTRY: PROBLEM SOLVED?

Chapter 7 — Goff

Health Reform, a national effort to address the deficiencies in healthcare and its escalating costs, finally culminated in the passage of the Affordable Care Act (ACA), affectionately or derisively referred to by many as Obamacare.

What could possibly go wrong?

> The question that was not asked

Winston Churchill, a great observer of America, was quoted as saying; "You can count on America to do the right thing, after everything else has failed." Which leads to the question being debated: Is Obamacare a failure, or is it the right thing?

Actually, that's the wrong question. The question that was not asked — and should have been *before* creating Obamacare as the solution — is this: "What is our nation's health policy, its priorities, and its valuation of services and capabilities?"

That debate would have been essential to obtaining a national consensus about what are the most important services and priorities within the American healthcare system.

Let's use pre-natal care as an example. Is it more important than elective cosmetic surgery? Another example: Are immunizations more necessary than hospitals?

Difficult questions. America doesn't seem to do well with difficult questions. One of the questions: "How do we intelligently spend our tax dollars?" While there is an attempt to deny this reality, there is a finite amount of money available. It's even worse than that. The general attitude toward the range and provision of healthcare services in this country could be characterized as "Everyone wants everything, but no one wants to pay for it."

Vast medical resources are at hand: Providers of the services, hospitals, physicians, and medical-device and supply companies. All benefit economically from delivering their services and products. The patient derives the benefit of better health, well-being and extended life — at least in theory.

Unless you take time to question and rank both services and needs, unless a consensus is reached about what is most important for funding, there will never be a national policy that then can be converted into a sustainable health benefit plan. A clear consideration of the efficacy of the service capable of being rendered is required; not everything that can be done carries equal weight and importance.

As carefully selected treatment models are compared on the basis of their contribution to health improvement, the most efficient and effective could then become the standard of care.

The result of this could be a financing model which is acknowledged and respected for supporting needed care that is current *and* proven.

A 2004 study by Banarto, McLellan, Kagy and Garber reported that 30 percent of all Medicare costs go to covering the costs of the 5 percent of the patient population that dies each year. One-third of that cost occurs in the last month of life.[1]

Patients with chronic illness in their last two years of life account for some 32 percent of all Medicare spending, according to the *Dartmouth Atlas of Care*. This care is active and aggressive, and it comes with little extension in longevity. It rarely focuses on palliative care, which is care of pain and support of patient comfort.[2]

So, how about a national debate on this topic? We would have to talk about things that we don't like to talk about — death, and the limits of our ability to provide everything that everyone wants at that terminal point of our existence, not to mention how to pay for it, which brings up the question of public resistance to the closure of largely obsolete and duplicative hospitals.

I offer as proof the public resistance to pay more taxes toward Medicare and Medicaid, as well as the business community's growing frustration with the continuing escalation of health insurance premiums.

Rather than have the hard debate, there is a continual witch-hunt for someone to blame. Everyone could have everything, if only physicians, hospitals, insurance companies, and pharmaceutical firms would cooperate to avoid being burned at the stake.

It Is Always Easier to Find Someone to Blame

According to an Institute of Medicine report issued in 2012, America spent $2.6 trillion on health care in 2011. A third of that spending — a full $750 billion — did nothing to make anyone healthier.[3]

As examples:

- Missed opportunities in preventive care resulted in an additional $55 billion in spending
- Fraud: $75 billion
- Unnecessary services provided: $210 billion
- Excessive administrative costs: $190 billion
- Prices Too High: $105 billion
- Inefficient care delivery: $130 Billion

The excessive administrative costs mostly are tied to the operation of our hospitals. America leads the world in administrative costs accounting for 25.3 percent of total U.S. hospital expenditures — a

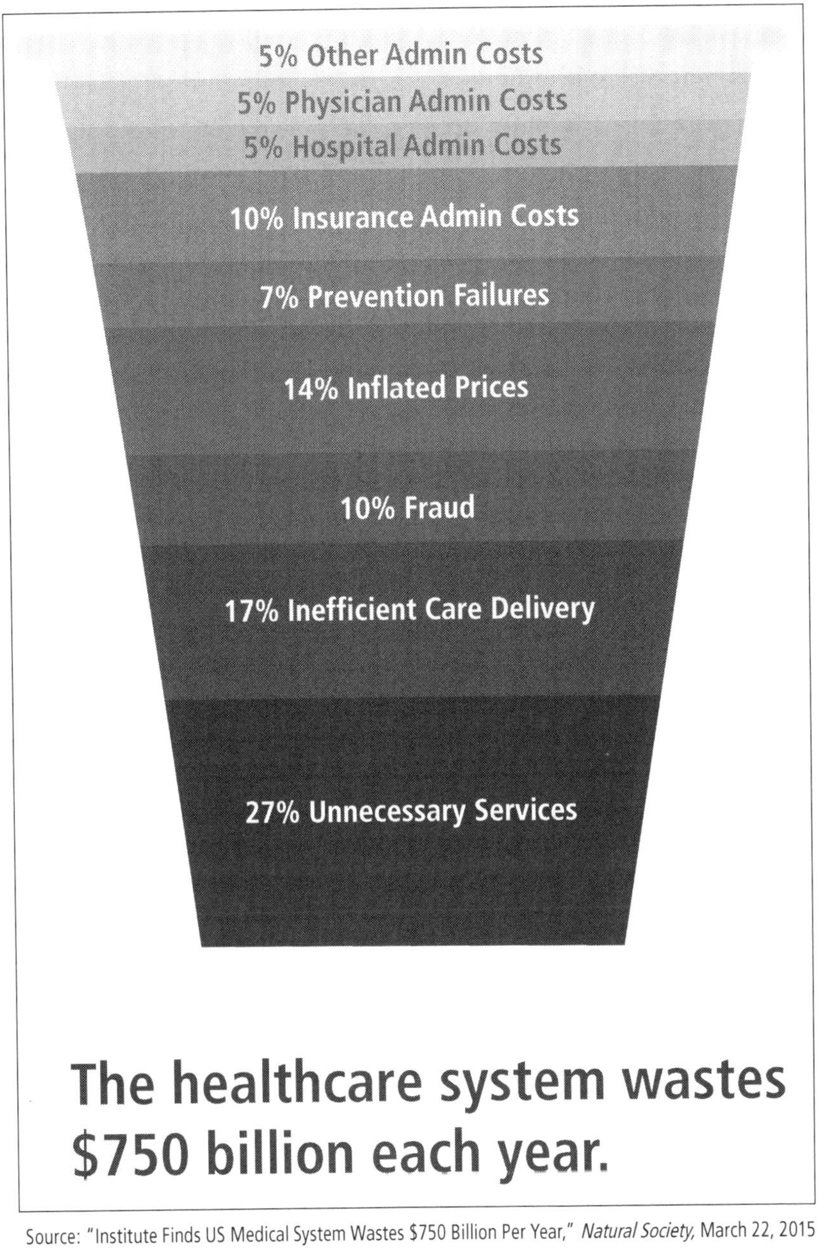

Source: "Institute Finds US Medical System Wastes $750 Billion Per Year," *Natural Society*, March 22, 2015

percentage that is increasing. Next highest were the Netherlands at 19.8 percent and England at 15.5 percent.[4]

Put aside the temptation to conjure up derogatory comments about thieving physicians, overpaid healthcare administrators, and hospitals for a moment. Ask if these people will only do what you and I want them to do — right? Well, *perhaps* — if enough of us make the agenda perfectly clear.

We need a national debate

A national debate *needs* to be undertaken to confront the overall greatest driver of waste in healthcare: The existing infrastructure. Once we have analyzed its (few) strengths and (many) weaknesses, we can then grapple with the costs and consequences of changing it — or not. Be assured that no solution reached will be cost-free, but it might be *cost-efficient.*

A great deal of waste exists because the infrastructure, our nebulous healthcare framework, is not a system that reflects current needs. It is the legacy of financing decisions made years ago, when we were dealing with problems that are no longer of concern. Back then, we could never have anticipated the problems we now face.

We flatter ourselves by claiming it to be "a system." To be a system, the process of treatment, costs and outcomes should be predictable for any given component. Yet if two individuals were to collapse on the street in different parts of New York City, it would not be possible to predict beforehand, with any accuracy, where each would be taken for treatment, what that treatment would be, what it would cost, and what the expected outcome would be. As such, this is not *a system.*

Our health-delivery structure is based on 19th and 20th century concepts and limitations.

The single largest cost-source of our healthcare "system" is the hospital. These sprawling, over-large bricks-and-mortar structures are the physical inheritance and embodiment of the needs of communities that came together to help the sick and injured with then-current technologies from 50 to more than 100 years ago. Among the most noble of enterprises is the community hospital, a collective response to the needs of a few and more often the poor.

An outdated health-delivery structure

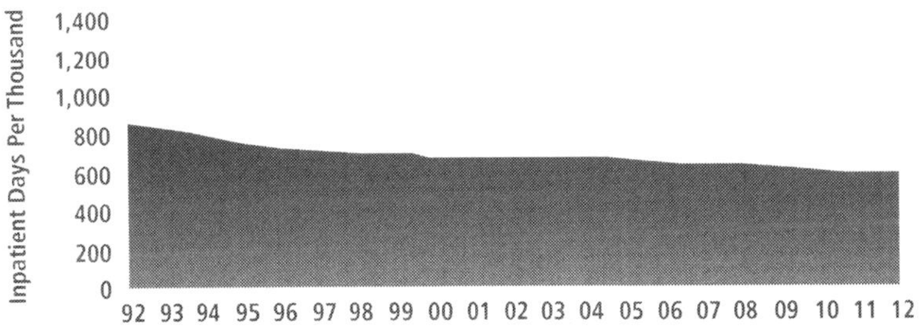

Inpatient Days per 1,000 Persons, 1992 - 2012

Source: *Trend Watch Chart Book 2014;* Chart 3.2, page 30, American Hospital Association

Back in the day, the demands of delivering care required centralized structures that had sufficient volumes of aggregated patients. How else could you afford the medical technology, surgical services, radiology, laboratory, and other costs at that time? How else could you protect a community from communicable diseases (many long since eliminated by immunizations)?

As modern and technologically sophisticated as they may be today, hospitals mainly serve as acute inpatient-care institutions, largely unchanged from their historic roots. Many beds are unneeded and unfilled.

The 19th and 20th century hospitals were created to serve communities that are no longer isolated by 20th-century roads and bridges. These hospitals often find themselves in the wrong location or concentrated in one part of a community or city, creating overserved and underserved areas.

Yet advances in medical-care delivery and in the treatment of injury and disease steadily reduce the need for the hospital. Cataract surgery, a delicate procedure, required almost a week of hospital stay 40 years ago. Today, this is an outpatient surgery; no hospitalization is required.

The evidence is all around us. Declining utilization is a trend that has been developing for the past five to 10 years. A multistate study conducted by Kaufman Hall indicated that inpatient-use rates per 1,000 declined significantly between 2006 and 2011. Declining use rates occurred for all age groups.

While the recession was blamed for this, a greater than 10 percent use-rate drop was for those aged 65 to 84 — whose healthcare costs are largely covered by Medicare — a signal that other factors are at work.[5] (See chart on page 107.)

The excess capacity of inpatient beds was graphically confirmed in New York City during the 2012 superstorm, Sandy. More than 2000 hospital beds, in the aggregate, were taken out of service in case of need Not one person died on the street as a result. Yes, there was inconveniences, like elective medical services being curtailed throughout the region.

> Beds reduced without increase in deaths

Still, 2,000 beds taken out of service clearly shows there exists excessive capacity. That excess capacity is a waste of our money. So, is the answer to get rid of hospitals? It's not that easy.

It's Not the Hospital — It's the People!

Hospitals are economic engines of their communities. They are large employers, and many have unions. When William DiBlasio based his NYC mayoral campaign in 2013 on a promise to fight the closure of two hospitals largely rendered unnecessary by improvements in more efficient care delivery, he won union support.

A little-noticed culprit is the disproportionate ratio of specialty-care physicians to primary-care physicians. Why are primary-care physicians more necessary to a balanced health system? They are the early-warning system; this is where problems are caught early-on, when they are more treatable. Without them, care opportunities are missed, and people require more specialized care.

That's expensive. Missed opportunities in preventive care represented $55 billion in waste in the Institute of Medicine Report mentioned earlier. However, they provide income and work for the medical specialists, their team, plus the larger staff and specialized facilities required.

This is not likely to change soon, given what's in the pipeline.

Physician Numbers Don't Add Up

From the 1960s to 2002, about 25,000 new physicians went into practice yearly, increasing the physician population at a rate of 3 percent, while the general population increased at only 1 percent yearly. While that may be seen as a good thing by those untutored in cost-benefit, the numbers don't add up for the rest of us.[6]

Today, an ideal healthcare system would consist of a balance of 70 percent primary-care doctors (internists, family physicians and pediatricians, as examples) and 30 percent specialists. We Americans have it backwards. We create a graduation class of 70 percent specialists and 30 percent primary care. This minority mostly feeds the majority, minnows feeding the whales.[7]

The value and contribution of the primary-care physician was well documented in a 2008 white paper by the American College of Physicians that reviewed the finding of 100 studies related to the form and substance of the role of primary care.[8]

That positive impact was on both quality and costs, reporting that an increase of one primary care physician per 10,000 in a state correlated to an increase in the state's quality rank by 10 places, a reduction in Medicare spending by $684 per beneficiary, and a reduction of 1.44 deaths per 10,000. The increase of one specialist correlated to a drop in quality ranking by 9 places and an increase in Medicare spending of $526 per Medicare beneficiary.

Again, the facts: 25 percent of the cost of healthcare is spent meeting the needs of 1 percent of the population, and 50 percent is spent on the next 5 percent.

Our healthcare delivery is a one-size-fits-all approach of bureaucratic controls trying to restrain use, when the focus should be on the early identification of these smaller portions of the population and facilitating their rapid access to the right physicians and care earlier on.

> 25% of healthcare costs go to the needs of 1% of the population

With this understanding as background, the deficiencies of Obamacare and health insurance can be more readily appreciated. Both provide for insurance and financial coverage for medical services as they are provided. Neither addresses the fundamental issues of a system that is out of sync with today's technology and population. They are not designed to address them, and they are not in a position to do so.

The Affordable Care Act, Obamacare, is all about giving people access to care, especially those previously precluded by their lack of insurance coverage. Health insurance is constructed to give people access to healthcare services by providing financial coverage.

To the extent the ACA removes that financial barrier, it can be considered successful. Similarly, to that same extent, the health insurance industry can be considered successful. Each is doing what it is designed to do. They both sorely lack the capacity and the will (even awareness) to address the issues of costs and waste.

The response to rising costs has not been a rethinking or redesign of the healthcare delivery system to provide an infrastructure and human resources appropriate for delivering care today. The response has been to squeeze the existing system.

The choice to date has been to starve the system in the hope the system somehow will find a way to do the right thing for people by unilaterally and wisely delivering care in a cost-effective and quality manner.

How Well Has That Worked?

It's a stretch to believe that institutions, including the medical community, whose first responsibility is for self-preservation, will voluntarily replace themselves with a more-efficient delivery structure. It's a further stretch to hope that medical schools will reduce the number of specialty training positions to the benefit of primary care.

An even-further stretch of credulity is to believe that hospitals will voluntary close and replace themselves with outpatient services and more community-focused services. Is there the political will to deal with the consequences of the major disruptions to jobs and communities that would result?

The step being taken in many communities is the merger of hospitals, the consolidation of services under one system or structure. However, what drags down delivering needed care in the communities is a desire to retain the same bricks-and-mortar structures that have existed for decades. A nagging question must be asked: Are these consolidations driving efficiencies or market control?

The mergers of hospitals and healthcare systems are more likely to lead to higher costs for consumers rather than more-efficient healthcare delivery, according to a Bloomberg opinion article.

"The disconnect between price and value has many causes, but the flurry of mergers and acquisitions in the preserving hospital industry is making it worse," Shannon Brownlee and Vikas Saini of the Lown Institute wrote in Bloomberg. "Hospitals command higher prices when they corner market share. They gain even more leverage when they gobble up large physician practices."[9]

As hospital enterprises capture market share and physician services, an example of the disconnect can be seen in the different pricing practices between physicians' offices and other community-based settings of care.

According to a study from the National Institute for Health Care Reform (NIHCR), average hospital outpatient department prices for common imaging, colonoscopy and laboratory services can be more than double the price for identical services provided in a physician's office or other community-based setting.

The average hospital outpatient department price for a basic colonoscopy, for example, was $1,383, compared to $625 in community settings. For a routine blood test — a comprehensive metabolic panel — the average price in hospital outpatient departments was about $37, triple the price of $13 in community settings.

The average price for magnetic resonance imaging (MRI) of a knee was about $900 in hospital outpatient departments (HOPDs), compared to about $600 in physician offices or freestanding imaging centers. Likewise, HOPD average prices for physical therapy were much higher than community settings. For example, a 15-minute unit of manual therapy was $58 on average in HOPDs, compared to $35 in community settings.[10]

Good Luck on Price Transparency

Because there is little price transparency before services are provided (when was the last time you saw posted prices for services?). Most patients discover the differential only when the bill is presented and their responsibility is revealed.

As an industry is being squeezed financially, just who is making the decisions, and how are decisions being made about the services that a community could or should be provided — or deprived? Is it for survival or good business that not-for-profit hospitals across America have reduced or shed unprofitable services and expanded or opened more lucrative businesses lines?

Do we encourage the creation or expansion of economically profitable walk-in urgent-care centers, ambulatory-surgery centers and so on, even when they duplicate those of a hospital a few miles away and siphon from that institution heretofore expected revenue? Should the hospital be relegated to providing services that are economically less attractive?

Consider the Pressures on Hospital Executives and Directors

Can a community expect hospital leaders, whose personal livelihood (paycheck) is based on the economic success of the institution in their charge, to make the decision to keep open a needed but economically unprofitable service? For example, mental-health services are less "margin contributing" than cardiac surgery. Should access be curtailed to mental-health care on that basis?

Healthcare now accounts for nearly 1 in every 7 dollars spent in this country. Any adjustment to the system to constrain its growth or re-direct and re-allocate that spending is bound to face tremendous opposition, as the financially vested interests are interlinked to protect the status quo.

No community wants to lose its hospital, and the economic consequences of such a loss are material and meaningful. The American Hospital Association reports that each hospital job supports about two more jobs and that every dollar spent by a hospital supports roughly $2.30 of additional business activity.[11]

Only a serious national debate resulting in an informed consensus will allow for a redesign of the medical delivery system and repositioning of the human resources appropriate for healthcare in the 21st century.

Do I need to remind you at this point that, in its absence, the vacuum is filled by politics and the blame game?

Why Change is Needed

Story #7

I'm sending this to hopefully see if at least this may work for my family. Since my mom's two strokes we have been piled up with bill after bill.

Well my dad and since he is the only one paying bills and we lost our house because we weren't able to pay mortgage, we now live in an apartment which is also difficult for him to pay rent.

I'm not writing for myself but I am asking to see if you could possibly help us out especially my dad to pay at least something from my mom's medical bills. I worry about this everyday since my mom got sick because he is the only one who is providing for this household since I attend college and have only a part time job.

Please. I would really appreciate your help, this would be a major stress reliever for my family. But if you cannot help it's alright regardless. Thank you for taking the time to read this.[12]

SENTENCED TO DEBT! CAN WE RE-THINK THIS?

Chapter 8 — Ashton

In spite of all the evidence provided, I'll bet that you are *still* itching to find someone or something else to blame for the state that we, you and I are in when it comes to medical debt.

Big Pharma? Insurance companies? Out-of-control medical costs? Physicians who prescribe every test possible to cover their tails? Private-sector and government "silos" that refuse to give up their power and influence, but use neither to solve our healthcare problems? Elected representatives who do *not* represent us but the heavy donors who couldn't care less about our well-being?

I'll make this easy. It's *you*.

Well, at least you, I and everyone who is involved in any aspect of this train wreck of a healthcare economy who isn't actively questioning the status quo and campaigning for change. And I mean even militantly so. Certainly, there are solutions. Take two aspirin and call me in the morning. Just put tab A into slot B, and everything will work better.

It's not that simple. Learn from your doctor: It is fruitless to treat *symptoms* and not address the *disease.*

Medical Debt is The Symptom — The *System* is The Disease

As much as I want to encourage you not to despair, in fairness, I must alert you that this subject may get personal. It may get uncomfortable. It may bring into question not only your own personal and ethical values but those of the country in which we live and the corporatocracy it has become.

Let's start at home base. How *you* choose to view debt will determine your personal success in managing this problem. This will start with your acknowledgement of your share of responsibility for bringing debt into existence (or helping others create theirs). The next step is to educate yourself (as you are doing now) about the players involved, sort out what works and doesn't work, and then take the steps that will lead to effective action.

Do you believe people should go into debt for medical expenses they did not elect to have, such as that liver ailment or that cancer treatment? (Let's put aside that face lift and tummy-tuck for the moment. Those are largely elective.) We are talking here about medical treatment ranging from a simple office visit and applying a cold compress up to cracking your chest to perform open-heart surgery.

It seems that we were promised better by the Founding Fathers. Does the "life" part in the promise of "life, liberty and the pursuit of happiness" not imply the right to receiving life-sustaining medical treatment?

> The problem is how we see the problem

The problem is not the "problem." The problem is the way we *see* the problem. The way we see the problem leads to the choices we make.

That's where it all gets sticky. Solutions to eliminating medical debt depend on the players involved. (*Spoiler:* The game is rigged.) Where are you and who are you in this scheme? Are you the doctor or hospital? The patient? The bill collector? The politician? The insuror? The lobbyist? Big Pharma? Union member?

Let's revisit ACA plans, again, for some clarification.

The Affordable Care Act, which was to usher in a new area of financial protections from the economic harm of illness, in itself can result in harm — unintended, but harmful nevertheless.

The **Bronze Benefit** Plans offered on the Health Exchanges carry $3,000 individual deductibles and $6,000 family deductibles with $6,360 maximum out-of-pocket costs, double that for a family, and a coverage package estimated to cover only 60 percent of the actuarially projected medical expenses.

The **Silver Benefit** Plans on the Health Exchange, the ones that must be selected to qualify for governmental premium subsidies, are based on a coverage page estimated at 70 percent of the cost of medical services and deductibles of $2000 for an individual and double that for a family.

The **Gold Benefit** Plans are based on actuarially projected medical expenses being covered at the 80 percent level and with a $1,000 deductible. If affordable, this is the plan to choose.

So, which did you — or will you — choose? Flip a coin? The most frequently chosen plans have been Bronze and Silver. How do the Insurers feel about this? Heads, they win. Tails, they win. Citizen complaints about this would fill another book.

Let's go back over the roles of the key players in this drama.

Physician, Heal Thyself

As a medical practitioner — You are immediately behind the 8-ball. You start out burdened by the cost of even *preparing* to go into business (i.e., medical school). Then, throw in the start-up cost of opening a medical practice: Equipment, payroll, staff, vendors, consultants, insurance, compliance. Oh, my.

The reward for that investment: *Some of the ingrates you helped aren't even paying you!*

As an unfortunate citizen/doctor in one of the few advanced nations that does not have socialized medicine, you will not have much of a say in costs and coverage. Granted, as Robert has pointed out, you can still expect to be successful because of the singular power of that diploma. (If you can call taking 10–20 years to pay off school debt being successful.) No wonder you have to charge so much!

Sadder yet is that medical school debt is only a fraction of America's overall burden of student debt. Reflect on those college friends who chose *not* to go to med school but other paths — comrades who will eventually become your patients one day. These graduates (and dropouts) collectively shoulder more than $1 trillion in debt from *their* student loans. Is it any wonder that they can barely make that co-pay, much less the deductible?

As a physician, what do you propose to do about that — or is that *their* problem?

So, let me empower you with a few pointers that will help you to maximize recovery, minimize loss, and incorporate both the *head* and the *heart.*

A shared lament among consultants and vendors in your industry is that doctors are their own worst enemy when it comes to creating unpaid medical bills. Few spend the time and fewer spend the money to put in place the requisite policies, procedures and technology. How is it that doctors go to medical school only to come out believing they are business school graduates?

Rule #1 — Have a policies and procedures manual to guide your staff, along with a one-pager explaining your payment requirements to the incoming patient. The first does not have to be a weighty tome but must clearly outline your policy regarding payments, late payments, use of credit cards, steps in the collection process, when and how to use third parties, or how to deal with an unhappy patient — or carrier. Your instructions to the patient must also be clear and simple. This is how the medical practice expects to be paid, and here are your obligations.

Rule #2 — Get a credit card on file with signed permission to use it for all medical-related billings. At the very beginning of the relationship is the time to discuss payment programs, not after your bill hits their kitchen table. Locate and utilize standard patient payment documents; don't reinvent the wheel.

Rule #3 — Verify patient eligibility and determine patient financial liability — and share that information with the patient! How much is that co-pay? How large is the deductible? When does insurance finally kick in? What can the patient anticipate paying out of pocket or over time? Both you and the patient need as much of a no-surprise relationship as is possible.

Rule #4 — Be compliant. If you use outside vendors for billing, be certain that they are PCI compliant — meeting the *payment card industry* (PCI) data security standard. All payment processors are required to meet a strict protocol.

Rule #5 — P, P and T. Be sure you have the proper and best *people, processes and technology* in place. It's a safe bet that your staff is not well trained in the interpersonal skills needed to work with an unhappy patient, or to ask for payment. It's also safe to say that your technology does not support collection activity (entering notes, payments, setting up and tracking payment agreements, generating carefully worded letters to motivate payment, mechanisms needed to transfer the accounts to agencies, etc.). Find experienced vendors to work with you; don't try this at home.

See? Simple as that — and every bit as complex. A great source of educational videos on the subject can be found at the website of www.EasyPayCollect.com, where you can ferret out even more tips and can explore the topics in depth.

As a patient — What plans do you have in place to deal with medical debt? Are you insured? Through a private carrier or with your employer? Do you live in a state that will not allow you to enroll in Obamacare? Is there any particular group that seems to have your health and financial well-being in their gun sights and aims to strip away what little protection you do have? Might that not be worth challenging?

If you do have insurance/Obamacare, have you considered carefully the options offered vis-à-vis pricing and level of service as outlined a few pages ago? Have you considered really carefully? Will that penny saved prove to be a dollar lost?

Are you presently in debt for past medical services? How much? How much of that is on credit cards or loans? How do you intend to meet these obligations? Will you be able to pay your deductible and still pay the rent? However small the amount, have you put money away for the unexpected and uncovered? Medical debt will become more troubling to those with borderline finances or junk insurance.

Our entire financial system — medical included — is based on a capitalism-gone-amuck, which requires continual feeding to sustain itself. Mega-sized entities operate much like the shark that can't stop swimming because it will die from lack of oxygen. If debt is *not* created, and the blood-oxygen of interest and penalties are *not* extracted, their entire ecosystem is in peril.

You cannot count on charity. Hospitals are rethinking their charity programs in view of the ACA. Many will accept the additional, expected burden, but some may well scale back help for those who *could have* signed up for coverage but *didn't*.

Don't count on "charity"

Peter Cunningham, a health-policy expert at Virginia Commonwealth University, presents a fair question. If a patient is eligible to purchase subsidized coverage and doesn't, should hospitals "provide charity care on the same level of generosity as they were previously?"

One hospital, Southern New Hampshire Medical Center in Nashua, NH, has placed this policy online: "Applicants who refuse to purchase federally mandated health insurance when they are eligible to do so will not be awarded charitable care."[1]

A further impetus is that the ACA is reducing payments for *uncompensated care,* the umbrella term for medical bills run up by patients clearly unable to meet their medical costs. The hospital is squeezed, tighter and tighter.

As the article describes it, the real question is whether a patient is unable or *unwilling* to pay for healthcare coverage.

"Did people choose not to enroll — or were they unable to get through the new health insurance marketplaces during the open enrollment in the fall and spring? Did they know subsidized coverage is available? Could they afford insurance, even with a subsidy, given that many insurance plans have deductibles that can run into thousands of dollars annually?" The article concludes with an observation by Mark Rukavina, a consultant to hospitals who is also a medical-debt expert.

"The big benefit from the health law is that it requires hospitals to make their charity policies public. The ACA's requirements will improve transparency dramatically."

The traditional way to escape medical debt has been through personal bankruptcy. It doesn't "abolish" the debt, but does render it *non-pursuable.* The downside is that, much like a scar, the debt will show on the credit report when bankruptcy is filed.

According to a 2013 study by NerdWallet Health, unpaid medical bills will continue to be the #1 cause of bankruptcy filings — surpassing both credit card and mortgage debt. Adding to the harm, a credit score will take a hit for up to 10 years.[2]

(Bankruptcy is the last thing that the bill collector wants to see you do, while, at the same time, it is their dogged and aggressive pursuit of those dollars that will drive you there.)

As a Debt Collector

On the bill collector's side, there are two participants: The debt buyer and the collectors and attorneys who purchase medical debt from that buyer. The latter's success lies in locating and contacting the errant patient and motivating payment, recovering on their investment and showing a profit. The former, profit dollars in hand from the sale, heads back to the hospital and larger practices to make more purchases. And on and on.

This is big business, so let's check out the statistics.

There are more than 4,000 active collection agencies in the USA employing nearly 450,000 people, and not one of them is publicly traded.

The largest agency is NCO (www.NCOgroup.com), which employs nearly 150,000 of these workers. NCO in 2012 reported $13 billion (!) in revenue. NCO not only receives "assignments" of bad debt directly from an original creditor, it is also a major purchaser of debt portfolios at deep discounts to pursue outstanding balances for their own gain, not for resale.

Conversely, the four major debt-buying companies are traded on the NASDAQ stock exchange. (You just knew the bankers had to be in there.) They are Asset Acceptance Capital Corp. (AACC), Asta Funding, Inc. (ASFI), Encore Capital Group (ECPG), and Portfolio Recovery Associates (PRAA). That may give you a clue about how much money is in this side of the business.

Of course, not all distressed receivables are medical, but to remind you of what I said earlier, medical-debt portfolios comprise more than 50 percent of all collection activity in America. Agencies know that. Debt buyers and sellers know that. Few doctors or patients know that.

As Robert has pointed out earlier, the Affordable Care Act won't be of much help against all medical costs. The problem does not lie in what the insurance will cover. It lies in everything related to those bills that insurance *won't* cover that puts the patient underwater. The drivers here are out-of-pocket costs for co-pays, co-insurance, travel to and from the doctor, lost wages, and high deductibles.

Every month the bill collector waits for a new infusion of fresh accounts to pursue. They are not "fresh" by most standards, even in our industry, but are newly in the queue. (As proposed legislation against collection abuse is causing hospitals to throttle back on their internal collections and extend payment pursuit timetables, they will arrive later and later. Sorry 'bout that.)

Traditionally, doctors and medical groups will grind away for weeks — even months — on non-responsive accounts in fruitless pursuit before they reluctantly place the accounts "out." But as I said, it's still a new account on *your* desk, the bill collector, and you have your own bills to pay. Hit the phones!

Let's give your industry credit for doing what you can to extract the last possible dollar for your medical client. You work hard, have the latest in automation, your collectors are motivated, and still you will recover no better than 8 percent of private-physician accounts and 12 percent of hospital accounts.

Let me put this another way. Your own industry statistics show that, on average, you will collect on no better than 10 percent of the dollars assigned.

Which introduces the dark secret of the collections industry. What happens to the 92 percent or 88 percent that remains uncollected? After hammering on them for weeks and months, you will now consider selling the unresponsive accounts to the next agency or a debt buyer.

Never Let a Dime Escape

Uncollected accounts can be sold and re-sold from agency to agency, and each time at highly discounted rates. Each new buyer aggressively attempts to collect on them at the original, full face value, along with freshly tacked-on collection fees and interest, which result in totals that often dwarf the original amount owed.

> Medical "Zombie" Debt never dies

Zombie Debt continues to rise from the write-off columns. It becomes debt that only grows and never dies. Our country's laws allow for that. Sadly, unlike the movie versions of battles with zombies, the story never ends happily in real life.

Nothing in the collections industry better exemplifies and defines this greed than the robo-signing, robo-calling mills that grind away to recover these dollars.[3] Apologists for the industry defend the sale of old, even out-of-statute debt (the time in which the debt can legally be brought to court) .

"Debt buyers play an important role in the economy, in that they recover rightfully owed consumer debt," said Mark Schiffman, a spokesman for the trade group Association of Credit and Collection Professionals (ACCP). He continues, "Companies and government rely on the repayment of credit, fees, services to keep their business functioning, and debt buyers help companies offset some of the unpaid accounts they incur. Selling accounts to debt buyers also helps banks reduce losses from lending money, which maintains the flow of credit at low rates."[4]

Publicly traded debt-buying giants Encore Capital and PRA Group announced financial results for 2014 that put them into the rarified "billion dollar" industry category. Encore marked a 39 percent increase in revenue over the prior year, and PRA's hike was similarly eye-popping. However, as the industry trade publication, *InsideARM,* reported in early March 2015, both companies were also being dogged by CFPB investigations.

Billion dollar giants

The online magazine describes PBA's annual report and call with investors: "PRA noted that its discussions also involved matters on which the company and the Bureau did not see eye-to-eye, saying, 'the CFPB has taken positions with respect to legal requirements applicable to debt-collection practices with which we disagree.'"

You had better hope that the CFPB wins that disagreement.

Of the more than 5,500 hospitals in America, 500 or so sell patient accounts to debt buyers, and for understandable reasons. They need to get it off the books, and they need to realize *something* from their own collection efforts and costs. Selling off $100 million in bad debt will realize a $1 million cash infusion.

What is the one good reason that more hospitals don't sell their bad debt? It takes only one aggressive-debt-collector story throwing the greedy hospital in with the "bad guys" to reach the local newspaper to cause blow-back. Both doctor and hospital are lumped together in the glare of community disapproval.

Why Change is Needed

Story #8

> *My sister has no email address of her own, so anything needed by email should be sent to me, her sister. I cannot even estimate the amount of debt owed. She has had so many hospitalizations, doctor visits, and lab work.*
>
> *She is making monthly payments on a number of them, so if those payments, in addition to everything else she owes, could be eliminated, it would be a tremendous hardship lifted off her shoulders.*
>
> *I would be eternally grateful. If you were able to help her!*[5]

MEDICAL DEBT: THE END, THE BEGINNING OF THE END, OR MORE TO COME?

Chapter 9 — Goff

In earlier chapters, I have endeavored to take the blame game out of the issue of medical debt, to remove the easy targets of physicians, hospitals and insurers. There is an essential way to set the stage for a search for workable solutions. When any discussion gets caught up in the fevered search to assign blame, facts become secondary, politics or self-survival becomes a priority, and any resulting solution is unsustainable.

> The fevered search to assign blame

One truth will remain. The financial impact of accidents and illness on individuals and families is not going to disappear magically now that Health (insurance) Reform has occurred. It is an ongoing public issue, and it will get worse. This conclusion is supported by two realities:

First, the advent of Health Reform does nothing to alleviate current *existing* medical debt. This burden is going to haunt people for years to come.

Secondly, Health Reform did not make medical services *free,* nor did it fundamentally change the delivery of care to make it more affordable.

In fact, while Health Reform makes health insurance accessible by way of eliminating pre-existing conditions and providing income-level economic support to subsidize premiums, consumers remain responsible for a large portion of the cost of their care.

A report by TransUnion, a credit and information company, found that between 2011 and 2012, the average patient out-of-pocket costs for healthcare grew almost by 22 percent in one year. The average deductible a consumer pays increased by more than 154 percent, from $405 to $1,032, and the average co-pay increased from $65 to $117.

While Health Reform should be deeply appreciated for removing the specter of catastrophic medical bills for most, it actually creates a potentially bigger problem, a mixed blessing of sorts. Medical debt incurred even under Health Reform will remain very disruptive for people, yet not large enough to trigger bankruptcy — which is the only current manner by which one can actually seek *full* relief.

Up to this point in history, most bankruptcy horror stories involve medical scenarios necessitating unexpected, extensive and costly treatment, whether covered by health insurance or not. Hopefully, the ACA will remove this burden. What it does *not* remove is the escalating share of the financial obligation that is still to be borne by the patient.

While that responsibility has an annual "cap" on the amount that the patient is responsible to pay, most caps are high enough to create a menacing level of impoverishment. This has not been taken into account by anyone. While people are assured that they will enjoy protection from a catastrophic health event, they are also being given a false sense of financial security. Allow me to elaborate by using an earlier example.

The most popular health plans offered under ACA reform can carry with them maximum out-of-pocket costs of $6,350 for an individual and up to $12,700 for a family. Those products carrying lower out-of-pocket maximums also carry higher premiums. As most people think from their pocketbook, you can expect that individuals and small businesses using the Health Exchanges are price sensitive and will seek out the policies with the "best" premium.

Herein Lies the Problem

The New America Foundation reported in 2009 that savings in the households of American families that are the intended beneficiaries of Health Reform are easily wiped out in their entirety by medical claims not protected under most policies sold on the Health Exchanges.

- Families earning $12,300 have only $1,700 in total savings and just $800 in transaction accounts (liquid assets) to weather emergencies.
- The three lowest income quintiles, with median incomes of $12,300, $28,800, and $47,300 have an average of $800, $1,600 and $2,700 held in financial-transaction accounts, respectively.

Please note that the median income of $47,300, with just $2,700 in financial assets available, compares with a national household income in the United States of $44,389 as of 2004.

In more personal and human terms, a survey, *National Survey: Privately Insured in America: Opinions on Healthcare Costs and Coverage,* by the Associated Press-NORC Center for Public Affairs Research Press, reported in October 2014:

- One in eight adults ages 18 to 64 with private health insurance would face major financial hardships, such as going without food or using up all of their savings due to medical bills.
- Among those covered by high-deductible health plans, almost 1 in 4 said that paying for healthcare caused them to use more of their savings.[1]

The Federal Reserve's 2014 Survey of Household Economics and Decision Making found that 47 percent of American households would have difficulty coming up with just $400 in the event of an emergency, without selling some household asset.

Returning to my original warning, policies on the Health Exchanges will keep you from bankruptcy but will devastate your family's finances short of needing that rescue. You will essentially trade in long-term chronic pain for excruciating but short-term pain.

Not considered in this economic meltdown is that a family is economically impacted by more than just the cost of medical services when illness strikes. Wage-earner incomes diminish — or even disappear. Family-member caregivers must adjust their own work to provide care. Who is caring for their other dependents or their children?

It gets worse. (Do I repeat myself?)

Adding Injury to Insult — Deductibles

Exposure to the continuation of medical debt and the ravages that it can cause is not limited to people who have found health-benefit coverage on the Health Exchanges.

Corporate America has followed the lead of Health Reform to implement deductibles into the group health-benefit policies offered to their workforce. These deductible levels are similar to those of products offered on the Health Exchanges, and at times they are larger. In the corporate world, deductibles up to $10,000 are not unknown — regrettably.

The concept of deductibles for insurance is almost as old as insurance itself. They have precedents in the property and auto insurance industries to ensure that a policyholder takes some financial responsibility for submitting a claim. This restrains the submission of smaller claims and also motivates policyholders to maintain their property and drive responsibly. The fees sting but are largely manageable in proportion to the anticipated cost of repair.

The deductible as a financial hazard

In health insurance, deductibles are not a practical deterrent to restrain unfettered utilization of services. In truth, they serve to obstruct the optimal use of medical services. Granted, co-payments can cause a patient to think twice before running to the physician for self-healing lumps and bumps. But the larger deductibles in health insurance serve to shift the cost of needed medical care to the patient; it does not deter a frivolous response to cancer or the sudden onset of appendicitis.

The deductible is a financial hazard caused by an uncontrollable event.

The ACA is an Attempt at Insurance — Not Healthcare — Reform

Health Reform, aka Obamacare, is an attempt to address the need for the larger population to access medical insurance, and it does that. What it does not do is reform healthcare — or even health insurance, for that matter. It is another stopgap approach to a real problem.

I cannot emphasize enough that Obamacare, while it will result in fewer bankruptcies, will still provide a false sense of relief and financial protection from medical costs.

As long as there is patient financial cost sharing, there will be medical debt.

Should there *be* patient cost sharing? In its absence, unnecessary, unfettered medical demand will not only drive up costs but contribute to a decline in the ability of people with more pressing medical needs to access care. However, the deductible, in particular, needs to be seen for what it is — a ransom to be paid before the protections of health insurance kick in. One more burden piled on the patient.

In summary, the greatest potential for reducing medical debt is to reduce the cost and delivery of medical care. But to do so, to achieve meaningful improvement in the underlying cost of medical care and its quality, there needs to be a widespread restructuring of the systems that deliver healthcare services.

In the absence of that, the discussion of the cost of medical care, the reason for medical debt, will be a debate about who is going to pay and how care is to be funded, and it will continue to miss the fundamental, root cause.

Why Change is Needed

Story #9

I was involved in a hit and run accident on my motorcycle in 1998.

I was rushed to Bellevue Hospital in New York City where over a 9month period I had 3major and 1minor surgeries. I broke most of my bones on the left side of my body, but the most severe damage was on my left elbow and upper arm. I also had major head injuries and lost my radial nerve on that same arm.

Almost 10 years after the accident…I went to (a hospital) to have a metal plate that was installed in my left arm/elbow removed. My body started rejecting the metal plate. (My doctor) had a hand specialist assist him with this surgery and in October 2014 over 6 years after the surgery I started receiving collection letters demanding $159,714.

(One doctor) is asking $80,000 of this amount and he was there just as a precaution if anything went wrong with my radial nerve. I am receiving endless calls which have me so stressed that I have problems sleeping. I been working since I was 15 years old and always stayed away from making unnecessary bills. I had excellent credit unit this expense came up.

I'm not looking for RIP Medical Debt to pay this bill for me. I will appreciate if RIP Medical Debt can negotiate a reasonable amount that I will be able to pay, so I can get my life back together.[2]

GOT MEDICAL DEBT? LET'S ABOLISH IT

Chapter 10 — Ashton

"At the end of every seven years you shall grant a release of debts. And this is the form of the release: Every creditor who has lent anything to his neighbor shall release it; he shall not require of his neighbor or his brother, because it is called the Lord's release"

(DEUTERONOMY 15:1-2)

If Obamacare can be considered a tsunami, in that its force surprisingly carried away almost everything opposing it, then the "Rolling Jubilee" (RJ) that was launched out of the Occupy Wall Street movement can be considered a 6.0 earthquake in the world of medical debt, medical debtors and the collections industry.

Only a small percentage of Americans are aware of the phenomenon called the Rolling Jubilee or its role as a game-changer in a business that largely operates in the shadows. Much like its Occupy parent, RJ seemingly came out of nowhere, even though the need for it was a long time brewing.

What is it? What are its origins? Why was it needed? Who fathered it? And even more importantly, *What does it mean to me and possibly to the future of medical debt*?

In mid 2012, Occupy's Strike Debt! working group purposely chose Rolling Jubilee as the name for a team commissioned with a formidable task: Raise $50,000 in donations from perfect strangers across America by way of live-streaming a one-time Internet fundraiser. Next, use these funds to go to the debt-buying industry and buy $1,000,000 worth of personal medical debt. The team then would abolish this debt. In full. Forever.[1]

This campaign of "people bailing out people," was a project that I initially dismissed when I first learned of it. Pointless! Abolishing $1 million in medical debt is a drop in the bucket within the debt-buying and selling market, where billions of dollars in medical accounts are bought and sold every year.

I told them so. Why even bother? It was patiently explained to me that I had missed their point of targeting medical debt, and I had.

"First, $1 million might mean little in the context of the medical and collections industries, but it will mean everything to those individuals or families who happen to be in our debt buy," one activist pointed out. (I expanded on this revelation in a *Huffington*

Post blog entitled, "Reflecting on Rescuing Stranded Starfish and Abolishing Medical Debt."[2])

"Secondly, the main thing we want to do is to bring to people's attention that *medical debt — on the face of it — should never exist to begin with*, not in a modern society that cares for its citizens!"

Medical debt should never exist

Well, both points made sense to me, and I offered, when asked, my many decades of industry experience to help in their early-stage strategies. While respect and confidentiality cause me to refrain from going into specifics and details, I will share my personal experience and thoughts about this extraordinary campaign and its soldiers.

I watched from the sidelines with keen interest as this all-volunteer team skillfully pulled together the campaign, an advisory board, a website, a 501(c)(4) corporation, and finally, a gala kick-off event over the Internet via streaming media.

That came about the evening of November 15, 2012, in a small but packed Greenwich Village night spot. The event consisted of entertainment provided by comedian Janeane Garofalo, *Daily Show* co-creator Lizz Winstead, and musical performances by members of Sonic Youth, Neutral Milk Hotel, TV on the Radio, and a number of other volunteer artists.

The team and the audience were both stunned by its success. RJ blew past the initial goal of $50,000 to raise *nearly* $200,000 *in donations* over the following weeks. That meant many times more than $1 million in medical debt could now be purchased and dissolved. Without additional fundraising campaigns or public solicitations, the money continued to flow in for months afterwards.

By mid-2014, RJ had raised more than $700,000 and purchased and abolished more than $25,000,000 in medical debt!

The press went overboard in its coverage, both positive and critical. The UK *Independent* found it to be a "scheme," in a good sense.[3] *Crooks and Liars* quoted liberally from RJ insiders Andrew Ross and Laura Hanna as they praised it.[4] The UK *Guardian* trumpeted its virtues, finding that it was actually "striking at the heart of Capitalism."[5]

Some Occupy insiders damned the project with faint praise.[6]

The Project Did Get Blessings, Perhaps Even From on High

The religious community, scholars and ministers could not but notice the project, intrigued by the biblical roots of the working group's name. They had no problem in recognizing the significance of this effort.

"'Rolling Jubilee' Cites Bible in Project to 'Forgive' Anonymous Debts," trumpeted a headline in *Christian Post* on November 16, 2012, and quoted liberally from a *Huffington Post* blog by Reverend Dr. Susan Brooks Thistlewaite.[7]

She declared, almost breathlessly, "What Jesus taught as a prayer about forgiving debt (Matthew 6:12) has just been operationalized by Occupy... Through prayer and deed, Jesus pursued an economic plan called the 'Jubilee.'

"Jesus starts his ministry (Luke 4:16-19) by standing up in the synagogue and reading from one of the texts of his Hebrew scriptures on the biblical 'Jubilee.' The biblical jubilee is a time of debt forgiveness and [*The Rolling Jubilee*] is exactly what Jesus was talking about and doing something about throughout his whole ministry."

In the summer of 2015, Rabbi Michael Lerner of *Tikkun* ran a major piece on debt. The need for reform and the importance — necessity — of debt forgiveness is central to many of the articles contributed,[8] as exampled by some of the article titles:

- "Jubilee on Wall Street: Taking the Bull by the Horns," by Shane Claiborne.
- "Reimagining Jubilee: A Political Horizon for Our Times," by Pamela Brown.
- "You Are Not a Loan: Strike Debt and the Emerging Debtors Movement," by Hannah Appel.
- "Debt Forgiveness: Who Owes Whom for What?" by Nancy Holmstrom.

Much to my honor, the rabbi requested my views to be posted as a featured blog, "Jubilee and Debt Abolition: A Bill Collector's Perspective."[9]

The rabbi sums it all up. "No system is perfect, and inevitably some will enrich themselves at the expense of others, and some will be placed under the domination of others. From time to time, we must be ready to make the necessary adjustments to bring freedom to all, in joy, peace, and common humanity."[10]

Not everyone shares this view — the majority being in the collection industry. From the debt buyer and agency's point of view, the intrusion of RJ into their world got mixed reviews. The industry online champion, *InsideARM* trumpeted "Debt Buyers May See Competition from Occupy Wall Street" and alerted its readers in the industry as to the "moles" in their world. (Hmmmm, as one of their featured bloggers around that time, I wonder who that might be?)[11]

> Rabbi: We must make necessary adjustments

In truth, they had little to fear — at the moment. If the idea of "people bailing out people" gains traction, however, they could find themselves outside the gates that they themselves erected. As I said in a *Huffington Post* blog at the time:

> Occupy's entry into this market and the approach it is taking will evoke a yet unknown degree of shape-shifting in third-party collections... one that is long overdue. At its best, its entry may even bring about corrections that many within its own ranks long have wished for — to

> rid themselves of "bad apple" debt buyers and agencies whose practices have led to public outrage and increased governmental oversight.[12]

A Decent Lineage, But What About Now?

In mid-2014, having succeeded in its mission, RJ decided to end its medical-debt-purchasing program, use its remaining funds to purchase and abolish student-loan debt, and open up a new campaign — this time centered on creating a debtors' union. There was no argument that RJ had made its case. In a civilized, industrial society, medical debt is wrong.

"Now that we have brought this to your attention, fellow citizen, what do you want to do about it?" That was the implicit challenge that led me to a question I had to ask myself. "Should this novel, and unexpectedly effective approach be abandoned?"

As an early fan of the program, I vicariously enjoyed the satisfaction from seeing people's medical debt wiped clean (or partly clean). In my heart, I could not let this campaign fade away.

So, where do we go from here?

Inspired by the Rolling Jubilee concept and successes, I reached out to Craig Antico, debt-buying expert (and personal friend), who had a depth of understanding and experience in the collections and debt-buying industry. He also was a fan of RJ.

Together, we decided to create a nonprofit and pick up the gauntlet. Robert Goff, the very first medical expert I introduced to the concept of debt abolishment and co-author of this book, was our next acquisition. He is now a board member.

On July 25, 2014, our New York nonprofit corporation, Medical Debt Resolution, Inc. dba RIP Medical Debt was birthed. Our mission: To seek out donations to help us locate, buy and abolish $1,000,000,000 — one billion dollars! — in personal unpaid and unpayable medical debt.

How far this project will have progressed by the time you read this book is unknowable, but we did launch a CauseVox fundraiser in early May 2015 and likely there have been one or two more by the time you read this paragraph.

There is the usual struggle to locate donors, personnel, offices, publicity, and marketing materials, and on and on. We can only hope our cause resonates.

Visit our website (www.RIPMedicalDebt.org) and stay up to date on our adventures and what effect we may be having on how people perceive and interact with medical debt, the collections industry, medical practices and legislation. Oh, yes, and please do press the "Donate" button.

We would be honored if you choose to join us to help us accomplish our stated goal — to buy and then abolish $1 billion in personal unpaid and unpayable medical debt.

Let's make this *all* of our jobs — abolishing medical debt. For good.

Care to engage in a random act of kindness?[13]

Why Change is Needed

Story #10

I became ill four months before becoming eligible for Medicare benefits. I had no medical coverage at that time. The debts from this illness are overwhelming and I doubt I will pay them in my lifetime.

I am 65 years old, collect social security and have a small part time job to help pay living expenses. I would like to continue working. The illness is progressive and needs maintenance care to prevent life threatening events such as heart attacks and strokes. At this time the surgeon's bill is in collections, so I cannot go for follow-up tests. There are also bills from two emergency rooms, a seven day hospital stay and various doctors and radiology.

My income is in the $20,000–24,000 range, depending on my health. I wish to remain healthy and be able to meet my obligations. These debts are making it impossible. I am considering bankruptcy for these reasons.[14]

TELL ME IF THIS HURTS

Chapter 11 — Goff and Ashton

Goff Digs Deeper — Why Is There Medical Debt?

Why is there medical debt?

The easy answer is that medical debt exists because of an unwillingness of this country, as represented by our political structure, to make health services universally available without cost.

Why is there this unwillingness?

There are two reasons. First, the cost, which begs the question of who is going to pay. Secondly, an underlying belief that one's health is largely dictated by their lifestyle. Health is the responsibility of the individual. Ill health is the punishment for those who do not take that responsibility.

What Jerry and I have stressed in this book is that the cost of healthcare, whether it is covered by one's insurance or not, is in reality a cost that is being borne by the entire population — no matter its source.

To the extent that an employee is fortunate enough to have health insurance benefits, that cost generally is being paid by their employer. If their benefits are through Medicare or Medicaid, then they are paid largely by taxes. Since we as a society are not prepared to let people without insurance die on the streets, those costs are being built into the prices charged, in subsidies to health care providers, (like hospitals and clinics for the poor), or to individuals — if they still have a penny to their name.

For those without the resources to pay in full, the medical debt created often becomes bad debt. This is as inevitable as the sun coming up in the morning.

What is occurring is a very sophisticated game of "How can I shift the cost to someone else?" If only my employer would pay more, if only government would pay more, if only someone else would do something so that I can pay less.

Healthcare access has a long history of being a political issue. It is an issue that early on separated the rich from the poor, and still does to some extent. However, healthcare as a cost crisis began to reach public and political awareness in the 1960s.

This became apparent as costs have skyrocketed, largely the result of an effort to improve access to care for those over 65 with Medicare, and for the poor with Medicaid. This narrowed the gap between the haves and have-nots, but it swelled the nation's healthcare bill to be paid by the general public.

Another Way to Look at This

The additional billions of dollars that became available to pay for medical care for the old and the poor stimulated massive investments in research and expansion of health services. All this has resulted in an expanded ability to restore people to health and keep people alive.

Prior to these two programs, the old and poor were expected to die — quietly and inexpensively.

The End State Renal Disease Program is an example of expanding access to life-giving care that benefits a larger segment of the population. It not only increases costs but unwittingly protects the status quo. The effect is to impede improving both quality of care and cost reduction found in newer, competing models. (Prior to 1972, kidney failure was not covered by Medicare. At that time and for many years, it was common for health insurance plans to have lifetime economic caps on benefits.)

With most renal failure occurring prior to age 65, there was limited money for treatment and little motivation to support the development or manufacture of dialysis machines and other treatments. An individual under 65 with kidney failure often quickly reached the lifetime caps of their health insurance, be it $250,000 or $1,000,000.

Individuals suffering from kidney failure were expected to die. In 1972, when President Nixon signed the bill providing for

Medicare coverage of renal failures, there were only 10,000 people on the treatment. Only the wealthy could afford to stay alive.

By 2006 more than 350,000 people were on dialysis, and the cost was over $8.6 billion. Today, the treatment of renal failure has become big business, with 60 percent of dialysis centers being owned by two large publicly traded companies.

Alas, now comes the argument/question: *Are the financial interests of today's healthcare businesses hampering the development of lower cost care?*

In a 2009 article in *USA Today,* Christopher Blagg, a University of Washington professor emeritus who for many years served as director of the Northwest Kidney Centers in Seattle, stated that about 30 percent of U.S. dialysis patients are candidates for home treatment although only 8 percent now do it. By comparison, about 55 percent of dialysis patients in New Zealand dialyze at home, as do 30 percent in Australia and 20 percent in Canada.[1]

This is the same question raised earlier in this book, but in a different way. With the healthcare industry representing 9 percent of the total employment in the country in 2014, and 17.1 percent of GDP in 2013, there is a tremendous interest and effort to protect the status quo.[2]

To the extent that healthcare-the-business exerts greater influence over their industry, the resulting higher cost necessitates greater efforts to shift that cost to others. Some of those "others" are the individual.

Let's Not Forget Lifestyle Choices

A second reason that contributes to the creation of individual medical debt is a socially based reluctance by most to pay for the consequences of someone else's lifestyle choices. These people *should* pay their own way.

Consider: if people are protected (by having their medical bills paid) from the consequences of their lifestyle, where is the motivation to take responsibility for healthier choices? Alcohol abuse cost the U.S. healthcare system $85.8 billion in 1988. The tab for cigarette smoking totals more than $65 billion annually. Costs related to obesity now surpass $27 billion per year.

The American Medical Association has indicated that at least 25 cents of every healthcare dollar is spent on the treatment of diseases or disabilities that result from potentially changeable behaviors. Whether the cause is smoking, alcohol abuse, poor diet, lack of exercise, failure to use seat belts, or overexposure to the sun, preventable healthcare costs are the first complaint of many U.S. healthcare critics.[3]

Why should I pay for someone else's unwillingness to make healthier choices? People who voluntarily expose themselves to hazards should pay, shouldn't they? After all, this is a concept built into life insurance as well as auto insurance. Skydive, and your life insurance premium will be higher. Drive a race car, and your auto insurance ramps up.

Health insurance is not health risk exposure adjusted. The "out-clause" of health insurance, the ability to deny insurance coverage for "pre-existing conditions," has been eliminated by Health Reform.

From a Different Viewpoint

What may be required is a more enlightened view of humans and illness, especially including those that are "self-inflicted."

Rather than using the blame-the-victim approach, we need to recognize that engaging in many of the "poor" lifestyle decisions are related to genetics, which have been shown to be an important role in determining whether a person abuses alcohol.

How much is obesity the result of psychological factors or physiological factors, not lifestyle choices?

Smoking often starts as a result of peer pressure and is largely influenced by advertising and promotional campaigns that are as manipulative as they are relentless. Predictably, smoking then becomes an addiction, physiologically and psychologically.

According to Louis Sullivan, former secretary of the U.S. Department of Health and Human Services, every person in the United States pays $221 annually for the health expenses of smokers alone. "Cigarette smoking has an adverse impact on every American, whether or not he or she smokes. That $221 cost comes out of the pockets of smokers and nonsmokers alike, largely in the form of increased healthcare and insurance costs."

Among the poor, where there is a higher incidence of unhealthy lifestyle choices, research suggests that socioeconomic factors are great influencers.

How much of a role does economics play in pushing the poor into high-caloric, lower-cost foods? How about the absence of fresh vegetables in the inner city?

Inadequate education and information contributes as well to uninformed choices, almost all of which contribute to poorer health, higher treatment costs and exploding costs of medical interventions.

Here, we need to rise above blaming the victims.

Rather than use increasing personal financial responsibility as a barrier to seeking medical help or as a punishment for needing medical aid, *we need to shift the idea of personal financial responsibility from the point of treatment to the point of decision — using the tools of information and education to influence behavior.*

For example, according to a 1990 Congressional Budget Office Report, increasing the price of alcoholic beverages by 18 percent would lead to a 10 percent drop in demand and a corresponding decrease in alcohol-related health care costs.

A review in Australia of the research on increasing the tax on smoking reports, "Most studies found that raising cigarette prices through increased taxes is a highly effective measure for reducing smoking among youth, young adults, and persons of low socio-economic status," which are the most vulnerable populations.[4]

In addition to a positive impact on healthcare services demand and costs, a reduction in smoking brings benefits to employers though reductions in absenteeism, lost productivity, as well as reduced healthcare costs, estimated at $6,000 per year per smoking employee.[5]

Lifestyle choices that lead to increased level of chronic diseases such as coronary heart disease, cancer, stroke, diabetes, hypertension, obesity, and osteoporosis are preventable. The severity of illness is reduced through proper nutrition. Healthier diets might prevent $71 billion in medical cost, lost productivity and the value of premature deaths associated with these illnesses.[6]

The lack of education and information should be a challenge to correct. Nutritional education — with a dash of home economics — is needed.

Likewise, an enlightened approach would be to provide financial incentives to support a healthier lifestyle, a positive incentive, rather than the penalty of increasing the individual's economic hit when they access healthcare services.

Some employers are trying this approach, not only by offering healthier living programs, such as smoking-cessation programs, but also increasing or decreasing employees' contribution to their health benefits for smoking or not, or maintenance of a proper weight. Such approaches need to be tried on the greater population.

The best way to avoid illness may be more carefully selecting your parents. Since that is not possible, accept that many have genetic predispositions to certain illnesses. An individual's potential to experience cancer, diabetes, cardiovascular disease, and asthma are all heavily influenced by a genetic predisposition.[7] Therefore, using increased individual economic responsibility for health care costs as a punishment for poor lifestyle choices is not a reasoned approach to genetically-based diseases.

Adding to the potential of a genetic predisposition are the environmental factors of living in a modern society that impacts the health of the population. Air and water pollution plus chemicals in manufactured materials and foods are beyond the control of the individual, despite trying to live a healthy lifestyle.[8]

While there is no question that lifestyle has a great impact on an individual's health status, it must be understood that genetics and the environment, along with the consequences of a modern world, all contribute to the health status of people, and passing the costs of medical care to victims is to shift costs to the unfortunate.

Medical debt is the expected result when those so victimized do not have the economic resources to carry that cost.

Still in support of the status quo, are you?

Ashton Points Out The Obvious — *It's NOT The Symptoms*

Sometimes, it's the obvious that is the most painful. When it is *not* obvious, consider it a shell game keeping us distracted.

I have no better way of pointing out that we are so mesmerized by the *symptoms* of a malfunctioning medical system that we are not paying attention to its *cause*. My share of this final chapter intends to provide perspective and even antidotes. Be sure to let me know if this hurts.

Greed is NOT Good

Contrary to the lecture given Teldar stockholders by Michael Douglas as corporate raider Gordon Gekko in the original *Wall Street* movie, greed is *not* good. Gekko suggested that a by-product of his greed would benefit Teldar stockholders. In a way, the speech prophesied today's versions of Gekko's greed but writ much larger.

Although not described that way in corporate brochures, untrammeled Darwinian capitalism is acceptable in that its results will benefit America's shareholders, which in the main, it turns out, are largely the famous "1%" so vilified by the Occupy Wall Street protesters.

Criticism of today's "Gekko" economics neither began nor ended with the "Occupiers." Here are a few current examples of those taking more than fair potshots at the financial elite:

Pope Francis, while on his famous visit to the United States, made a point to deplore the economic disparity between the haves (so few) and have-nots (so many). He remarked on the poor:

"They are cast off by society, forced to live off what is discarded and suffer unjustly from the consequences of abuse of the environment."[9]

This Pope had been even more acidic earlier in the year by castigating the creators of poverty, those involved in the "unfettered pursuit of money" — or as he elegantly described it, the "dung of the devil." He urged the poor and disenfranchised to rise up against corporations, loan agencies, austerity, and "the monopolizing of the communications media."[10]

On the home front, we find another terrific example of outrage in Bernie Sanders, a major critic of Wall Street excesses. Describing himself as a Democratic Socialist, he has devoted a lifetime to campaigning against corporate influencers and their obscenely well-paid lobbyists.

Could it be that the Pope and Bernie were twins separated at birth? Well, definitely in a political and philosophical sense. *Time* magazine noted that of all the would-be candidates for President of the United States, Bernie Sanders' "political philosophy lines up most closely with the economic and social theories of Pope Francis. Healthcare as a universal right… economic injustices of income equality."

Bernie's take? "I'm not quite as radical as the Pope, but…"[11]

Both gentlemen have benefited from the emergence of Donald Trump as a Republican Presidential candidate. Who better to serve as the poster child of the 1%? But Trump is oddly compelling in that he has unloaded a few rounds on Wall Street. All the while, as one *HuffPost* blogger noted, "channeling" Occupy.

The Republican base rejoices in the fact that The Donald will not take political contributions and thereby cannot be bribed by (his fellow) 1 per-centers. What greater authority to confirm the evil of corporate influence than one who boasts of having invested some $1.5 million in politicians in the past? Trump makes it official: "When you give, they do whatever the hell you want them to do."[12]

However, let's return to this book's theme — the need for an Obamacare and medical debt collections survival guide.

How Greed Affects Health Care

Robert has touched on this subject throughout his chapters: greedy doctors, greedy hospitals, greedy carriers, greedy pharma, greedy-this-and-that, so I won't go over his well-documented specifics. Rather, let me highlight a few medical-industry "Gekkos" that I have identified.

In my opinion, the price-gouging drug CEO of the year, and perhaps the decade, is Martin Shkreli.

This former hedge-fund operator, through his firm Turing Pharmaceuticals, purchased the rights to the 62-year-old drug Daraprim and proceeded to raise its price from $18 a pill to $750 a pill — a 4,000 percent increase. This is a significantly important drug for people afflicted with a life-threatening condition called toxopasmosis, caused by parasitic infection, and the public response was particularly incensed. How can you justify this?

Shkreli set about to explain his reasoning through interviews on the major networks — bad idea, it turns out — by pointing out his logic. As he described it, the drug's price had been so low "that any company selling it would be losing money." At the new price there would be "a reasonable profit, not excessive at all."

He, like Gekko before him, pointed out the altruistic benefits of his intervention and the change in pricing. With the new profits, he declared that his company "could invest in researching a new drug for the condition." Reporters located medical experts who disagreed, saying the drug worked just fine and that no replacement was needed. Heavens! Where will these profits then go?

Shkreli's excuses were so poorly received that even the Pharmaceutical Research and Manufacturers of America — the drug industry trade group — felt compelled to respond on Twitter to its 33,000 followers to state that "@TuringPharma does not represent the values of @PhRMA member companies."[13]

This begs the question about what *does* represent their values? From what moral stand are they allowed to remark on the excesses of one of their members when in 2002 the combined profits of the ten drug companies in the Fortune 500 — $35.9 billion — were more than the profits for all the other 490 businesses put together? What moral stand can they take when figures show more money is spent on marketing and promotion than on drug research?[14]

As Sanders has pointed out, patients are paying for massive amounts of congressional lobbying — in 2014 alone adding up to about $65 million more than any other industry spent on lobbying. "Between big government's unwillingness to negotiate prices and its failure to fight fraud, it's no wonder drug prices are out of control," he complains.[15]

In contrast, consider the generosity of Dr. Jonas Salk who developed the anti-polio vaccine. Even though critics claim that he would have patented the Salk Vaccine if he could, the fact is clear that he declined to pursue patent ownership. In a television interview with Edward R. Murrow at the time, he was quoted to ask rhetorically, "Would you patent the sun?"[16]

Can you guess how many multinational corporations would do exact that with the sun's energy, if they could?

And in The Wider World of Greed

As I have asserted throughout this book, almost every industry is subject to manipulation by those whose financial self-interest trumps social — shall I say, moral — responsibilities. Even though the medium is different, the same factor is at work. Greed. Except we don't use that word. We call it, variously, "market forces" "return on investment" or "enhancing shareholder value."

Consider student debt.

Long before I was quoted on the front page of the *New York Times* in 2012 on this subject ("Debt Collectors Cashing In on Student Loans"), I had already been busy alerting anyone who would listen to me about the impending disaster of unpaid and unpayable education loans.[17]

Prior to Occupy's emergence, I wrote a blog in August, 2010 titled *"Campus Loan Predators: Get Out the Bait and Traps!"* — announcing that student debt had just surpassed credit card debt of $826 billion. I updated that column in October, 2011 with the horrific news that it had actually surpassed one *trillion* dollars. Today, it stands at around $1.3 trillion — and growing.[18]

When I was invited to blog for the *Huffington Post,* the very first article I posted on January 21, 2012, was "America's Financial Institutions and Student Lenders — Attention: OWS "Occupy Student Debt: Committee Has Something to Say."[19]

And today? That committee was absorbed into the larger working group, Strike Debt, and this body continues to lead the assault against big banks and governmental misdeeds. Their first venture, the Rolling Jubilee, became a major wedge into the consciousness of the American public.

On Occupy's third birthday on September 17, 2014, I blogged that the Rolling Jubilee had gone to the debt markets to locate, buy and abolish $3,856,866.11 in student loans, unburdening 2,761 individuals and their families.[20]

Moreover, they declared the formation of a force even more formidable — a Debt Collective, which is proving to be a major thorn in the side of both nonprofit and for-profit colleges that they claim are taking unfair and usurious financial advantage of their students.[21]

What has been the finance industry's response to suddenly-awakened government attempts to institute payback plans to ease the burden of college loans? Here's a headline as a clue: "Debt Relief for Students Snarls Market for Their Loans." Much like mortgage-backed securities (and we know how well that went), banks profit by selling off or repackaging student loans into bonds.

With Moody's and Fitch Ratings collectively placing more than $36 billion student loan packages on watch for a likely downgrade — you can imagine the disappointment in Wall Street. Do you remember the childhood game around of the early 1900's — Hot Potato?[22]

I could go into any number of government-sanctioned businesses and business practices that in any civilized society would be called extortionate at best and rapacious at worst — like payday lending with annual interest rates of 391 to 521 percent.

Framed as an easy way to tide over a borrower until the next paycheck, in practice payday loans "roll over" to keep the average borrower in debt for an average of 212 days a year, according to the Religious Action Center of Reform Judaism.

Their studies show that 12 million Americans are unable to escape this cycle of payday loans, "perpetuating further cycles of economic inequality and locking Americans into poverty. Indeed, those who borrow payday loans are more likely to have overdraft fees leading to closed bank accounts, *unpaid medical bills* [italics mine], credit card delinquency, and even bankruptcy.

"Relying on payday loans leads to other issues that are symptomatic of economic inequality, demanding that we work to address these issues in promotion of economic justice," their blog declares.[23]

Auto title loans, anyone? Almost 8,000 car title lenders operate in 21 states, charging borrowers $3.6 billion in interest on $1.6 billion in loans annually. Typically, a borrower will receive cash equal to 26 percent of a car's value. For that privilege, he or she pays an annual percentage rate of 300 percent.[24]

Oh, and should you default on that loan? You lose probably one of the largest assets you have, and you will also be hit with a $300 to $400 "repo" fee.

So, what does this have to do with our topic of medical debt? Everything, as everything in some way is connected.

People don't owe medical debt in a vacuum. To pay off that note, they or their caregiver must travel to a job. Losing the car may cost them that job — one more nail in the coffin.

Do you think it important to fill that prescription? Better stop by the payday loan joint today. Go again two weeks from now, or until you default on that loan, and they garnish the very same checks you are borrowing against to live on.

It's all of a piece. No one is sure which domino will fall first, but because the system rewards greed and excess, we as a society are screwed — and those dominoes *will* fall.

Except For — A Change in the Air

People are not taking it any more. They are stepping up in ways unimaginable to put their own lives and careers on the line to do that famous thing we call "make a difference."

I'll end this chapter with an example, one in which the *heart* and the *head* that Robert and I have been discussing have made a strong connection with each other.

Future Doctors Rising Up for 'Medicare for All'

What is said and how it is said are so important that I am including a quote directly from an article called "Future Doctors Rising Up for 'Medicare for All'" in the September 28, 2015, issue of CommonDreams.org.

> For most of us in medicine, helping people live healthy, happy lives is at the heart of why we chose this career. We expound upon this in application essays, talk about it during interviews, and start medical school with this "calling" fresh in our minds.
>
> Very early in our medical careers — on the wards and in the classroom — we learn that inequality, preventable illness and death are an inherent part of our current private, for-profit-oriented health insurance system.
>
> We see patients receive preventable amputations due to untreated diabetes. We see people permanently disabled by stroke because they were unable to afford their medications. College funds emptied out to pay for $100,000-a-year cancer treatments. Families bankrupted and lives destroyed.
>
> We learn that, although the United States is one of the wealthiest countries on earth, we are also the only

> developed nation that does not provide healthcare to all of its citizens. We learn that we spend more than 17 percent of our GDP — more than any country in the world — on this non-universal coverage. We learn that medical debt is the leading cause of bankruptcy in the United States.
>
> We learn that, despite its title, the Affordable Care Act is not truly affordable. Even after the ACA, tens of millions of people are still unable to afford insurance, and tens of thousands die every year because of uninsurance. Millions more who have insurance are under-insured, risking financial distress in the event of serious illness and finding that their health policy's high deductibles and co-pays prevent them from using it.
>
> All of which leads most reasonable medical students to ask, "What can we do about this?"[25]

I am going to ask the reader the same question. From *your* point of view, *your* career, *your* political persuasion, and *your* ethical construct. What can *you* do about this?

Your fellow Americans are dying to hear from you.

Why Change is Needed

Story #11

Approximate amount owed: $3,500.00. Thank you for creating this organization and helping others get out from under the burden of medical debt.

This is my reason for requesting assistance from your company: I'm separated from my abusive husband and having a hard enough time making ends meet from month to month without additional lingering bills weighing on me.

Normally, I'm the one giving to others and volunteering my time, but now, I must swallow my pride to ask for help myself. On top of it, I must repair my car so I can continue to have a way to get to/from my jobs and the volunteering that I do.

This medical debt is having a significant effect on my credit, which is preventing me from being able to finance a new(er) car so that I do not have the expense of constantly repairing my current vehicle.

I'm sure you hear all sorts of stories from people in need; I hope that the smaller dollar amount that I owe might be easier for your company to consider assisting with. I work in the healthcare industry so I see how much everything costs and I sympathize with people faced with medical bills far in excess of mine.

Please consider assisting me in getting this part of my life back on track so that I can get everything else in my life into a much more stable place.[26]

THE BUTCHER, THE BAKER, THE CANDLESTICK MAKER

Epilogue — Ashton

In the Prologue, Robert Goff offered an analogy to the evolution of our book by referencing our possible parallels to our favorite characters in *The Wizard of Oz,* the Scarecrow and the Tin Man.

Looking back on the work we invested in researching and writing this book, I can tell you that Robert definitely found his *mind* and I definitely found my *heart.* To be truthful, much like our Oz counterparts, we weren't actually missing these important organs when we started. We simply realized them more fully.

We both feel that the work you hold in your hand (or viewing on your screen) is essential to your arriving at a "solution by understanding." Dive deep into the ideas we present. As with us, it requires conscious work to connect your head and your heart.

I'd like to bring in another literary simile and take poetic license with an even more ancient literary antecedent to illuminate your understanding: "Rub-a-Dub-Dub."

Rub a dub dub,
Three fools in a tub,
And who do you think they be?
The doctor, the patient,
The bill collector,
All put out to sea.[1]

Further torturing Mother Goose, picture the "tub" as our government. "Out to sea" we are, insofar as our collective attempts to date in solving what argues to be the insolvable. It's time for us to look around this leaky ship carefully. Some of us are bailing as fast as we can, while others are busy drilling more holes.

As an aware crew member, you will need to make some hard decisions if we are going to get safely into port. You may have to take responsibility for helping with bailing. You may even want to determine who isn't rowing and might need to walk the plank. I invite you to actively prod them to take that stroll. This well-worn, but useful, quote applies: They are either part of the solution or part of the problem.

Robert and I challenge you to continue this education. Put on your thinking cap and formulate strategies to put this information to work, engage your heart, and then set out to do what you are being called to do.

Make that fabled positive difference and leave our world a better (and less indebted) place than you found it.

Endnotes

Chapter 1

1 2013 Commonwealth Fund International Health Policy Survey. Commonwealth Fund. November 13, 2013. http://www.commonwealthfund.org/interactives-and-data/surveys/2013/2013-commonwealth-fund-international-health-policy-survey

2 Boyer, Ray, and Paul Colford. "National Survey: Privately Insured in America: Opinions of Health Care Costs and Coverage" Associated Press-NORC University of Chicago. October 13, 2014. http://www.apnorc.org/PDFs/Coverage/NORC-AP-NORC-Release-Privately-Insuredl.pdf

3 "84 Million People Were Uninsured for a Time or Underinsured in in 2012; Nearly Decade-Long Trend of Rising Uninsured Rates Among Young Adults Reversed." Press release. The Commonwealth Fund, April 26, 2013. http://www.http://www.commonwealthfund.org/publications/press-releases/2013/apr/new-health-insurance-survey

4 LaMontagne, Christina. "Nerd Wallet Health Finds Medical Bankruptcy Accounts for Majority of Personal Bankruptcies." *Nerd Wallet*. March 26, 2013. http://www.nerdwallet.com/blog/health/2014/03/26/medical-bankruptcy/

5 "2013 Employer Health Benefits Survey" The Henry J. Kaiser Family Foundation. August 20, 2013. http://kff.org/report-section/2013-summary-of-findings/

6 Rosenthal, Elizabeth. "After Surgery, Surprise $117,000 Medical Bill from Doctor He Didn't Know." *The New York Times*. September 20, 2014. http://www".nytimes.com/2014/09/21/us/drive-by-doctoring-surprise-medical-bills.html

7 Benson, Barbara. "Aetna Accuses NY Docs of Overcharging Patients." *Crain's New York Business*. February 7, 2012. http://www.crainsnewyork.com/article/20120207/HEALTH_CARE/120209916/aetna-accuses-ny-docs-of-overcharging-patients

8 Layton, Mary Jo, and Mindy Washburn. "Aetna Sues Doctors over Bills it Calls 'Excessive'." North Jersey.com. http://www.northjersey.com/news/aetna-sues-doctors-over-bills-it-calls-excessive-1.183270

9 Mourar, Mary (ed.). *Experts Answer: 95 New Practice Management Questions.* Washington, DC: Medical Group Management Association, 2011. Chapter 2. http://www.mgma.com/Libraries/Assets/Store/8369-Sample-Chapter.pdf

10 Coughlin, Teresa A., John Holahan, Kyle Caswell, Megan McGrath. "An Estimated 84.9 Billion in Uncompensated Care Was Provided in 2013; ACA Payment Cuts Could Challenge Providers." *Health Affairs.* 33, no. 5 (2014): 807-814. http://www.scribd.com/doc/226548224/Health-Affairs-journal-by-the-Urban-Institute-on-uninsured-patients

11 Hawkins, Merritt. *A Survey of America's Physicians: Practice Patterns and Perspectives.* The Physicians Foundation. September, 2012. http://www.physiciansfoundation.org/uploads/default/Physicians_Foundation_2012_Biennial_Survey.pdf

12 Coughlin, et al. Abstract. http://content.healthaffairs.org/content/33/5/807.abstract ; Moore, Rodney J. "Stopping the Rise in Hospital Bad Debt." *Healthcare Finance.* September 30, 2013. http://www.healthcarefinancenews.com/news/stopping-rise-hospital-bad-debt-0

13 "The Hospital Accounts Report Analysis on Fourth Quarter 2012." The Association of Credit and Collection Professionals. http://www.acainternational.org/products-healthcare-collection-statistics-5434.aspx

14 *Medicare and Medicaid Research Review.* https://www.cms.gov/mmrr/index.html

15 Herman, Bob. "18 Hospitals that Closed in 2013." *Becker's Hospital Review.* January 2, 2014. http://www.beckershospitalreview.com/leadership-management/hospitals-that-closed-in-2013.html

16 "CBS News, New York Channel 7, 7/17/15" *Seen at 11: A Phone Call From Collectors That Can Actually Get You OUT Of Debt.* http://newyork.cbslocal.com/2015/07/17/seen-at-11-a-phone-call-from-collectors-that-can-actually-get-you-out-of-debt/

Chapter 2

1 "NCO Financial Systems." Collection Agency. http://collectionagency.info/reviews/nco-financial-systems/

2 Unnikrishnan, Deepak. "Spiralling Debts and Shame Drive Dozens of Indians to Suicide in UAE." *The National.* October 30, 2013. http://www.thenational.ae/world/south-asia/spiralling-debts-and-shame-drive-dozens-of-indians-to-suicide-in-uae#ixzz3KOSKJp4q

3 Woldow, Diana. "Clearing Cafeteria Debt without Shaming Children." *Beyond Chron.* February 10, 2014. http://www.beyondchron.org/clearing-cafeteria-debt-without-shaming-children/

4 "U.S. Total National Debt." The Concord Coalition. http://www.concordcoalition.org/us-total-national-debt

5 "CBS News, New York Channel 7, 7/17/15" *Seen at 11: A Phone Call From Collectors That Can Actually Get You OUT Of Debt.* http://newyork.cbslocal.com/2015/07/17/seen-at-11-a-phone-call-from-collectors-that-can-actually-get-you-out-of-debt/

Chapter 3

1 "New AMA Study Reveals Majority of America's Physicians Still Work in Small Practices." AMA News Room. July 8, 2015. http://www.ama-assn.org/ama/pub/news/news/2015/2015-07-08-majority-americas-physicians-work-small-practices.page

2 "Total Professionally Active Physicians." The Henry J. Kaiser Family Foundation. October 2015. http://kff.org/other/state-indicator/total-active-physicians/

3 Pourmassina, Linda. "The Vanishing Oath." *Pulsus*. November 17, 2010. http://pulsus.wordpress.com/2010/11/17/the-vanishing-oath/

4 "U.S. Total National Debt." The Concord Coalition. Fiore, Kristina. "On Doc Pay Release: 'You Cannot Call a Plumber for $57.'" *MedPage Today*. April 9, 2014. http://www.medpagetoday.com/PublicHealthPolicy/Medicare/45187

5 "AMA Resources for Medical Students." American Medical Association. http://www.ama-assn.org/ama/pub/medical-students/medical-students.page?

6 Diamond, Dan. "Why the Reports of the Death of Physician Participation in Medicare May Be Greatly Exaggerated." *The Health Care Blog*. August 6, 2013. http://thehealthcareblog.com/blog/2013/08/06/why-reports-of-the-death-of-physician-participation-in-medicare-may-be-greatly-exaggerated/;
Galewitz, Phil. "Study: Nearly a Third of Doctors Won't See New Medicaid Patients." *Kaiser Health News*. August 6, 2012. http://www.kaiserhealthnews.org/ stories/2012/august/06/third-of-medicaid-doctors-say-no-new-patients.aspx

7 See more at: Joszt, Laura. "Physician Reimbursement Dropped Sharply." *Physician's Money Digest*. February 2, 2013. http://www.hcplive.com/physicians-money-digest/practice-management/physician-reimbursement-dropped-sharply

8 Lowes, Robert. "Medicare Rates Continue to Fall Behind Practice Expenses." *Medscape*. August 29, 2013. http://www.medscape.com/viewarticle/810242

9 "Physician Practice Interactions with Health Plans Cost $31 Billion a Year, Equaling 6.9% of All Spending for Physician and Clinical Services, New Study Finds." Press Release. The Commonwealth Fund. http://www.commonwealthfund.org/publications/press-releases/2009/may/physician-practice-interactions-with-health-plans-cost-31-billion-a-year

10 Minott, Jenny. "Findings Brief: What Are the Costs to Physicians of Administrative Complexity in Their Interactions with Payers?" Robert Wood Johnson Foundation. 13, no. 2 (March 2010). https://www.academyhealth.org/files/publications/HCFOMarchFindingsBrief.pdf

11 Hawkins 2012. http://www.physiciansfoundation.org/uploads/default/Physicians_Foundation_2012_ Biennial_Survey.pdf

12 Mahon, Mary. "New Commonwealth Fund Report: 21 Percent of Adults with Health Insurance Spent 5 Percent or More of Their Income on Out-of-Pocket Health Care Costs." The Commonwealth Fund. November 13, 2014. http://www.commonwealthfund.org/publications/press-releases/2014/nov/out-of-pocket-costs

13 Cohen, Robin A., Renee M. Gindi, and Whitney K. Kirzinger. "Financial Burden of Medical Care: Early Release of Estimates from the National Health Interview Survey, January–June 2011." Centers for Disease Control. March 2012. http://www.cdc.gov/nchs/data/nhis/health_insurance/financial_burden_of_medical_care_032012.pdf

14 "CBS News, New York Channel 7, 7/17/15" *Seen at 11: A Phone Call From Collectors That Can Actually Get You OUT Of Debt.* http://newyork.cbslocal.com/2015/07/17/seen-at-11-a-phone-call-from-collectors-that-can-actually-get-you-out-of-debt/

Chapter 4

1 Rowe, Jeff. "Uncompensated Care an Ominous Trend" *Healthcare Finance.* June 2, 2011. http://www.healthcarefinancenews.com/news/uncompensated-care-ominous-trend

2 Kennedy, Tony, and Maura Lerner. "Accretive Is Banned from Minnesota." Star Tribune. July 31, 2012. http://www.startribune.com/accretive-banned-from-minnesota-for-at-least-2-years-to-pay-2-5m/164313776/

3 Shinkman, Ron. "Is Accretive Health in a Death Spiral?" *FierceHealthFinance.* March 17, 2014. http://www.fiercehealthfinance.com/story/accretive-health-death-spiral/2014-03-17

4 Albright, Evan. "Hospitals, Debt Collectors Rush to Create Standards for Collecting Patient Debt." *Forbes.* September 4, 2013. http://www.forbes.com/sites/insidepatient finance/2013/09/04/hospitals-debt-collectors-rush-to-create-standards-for-collecting-patient-debt/

5 "Key Facts about the Uninsured Population" The Kaiser Family Foundation. October 5, 2015. http://kff.org/uninsured/fact-sheet/key-facts-about-the-uninsured-population/

6 Garcia, Eric, and Garrett Lerner. *Repo Men.* Directed by Michael Sapochnik. Los Angeles: Universal Pictures. 2010.

7 The Editorial Board. "Alarming Abuses of Medical Credit Cards." *The New York Times.* October 19, 2013. http://www.nytimes.com/2013/10/20/opinion/sunday/alarming-abuses-of-medical-credit-cards.html?_r=0

8 "CMS Data Show Mixed Results from Medicare ACO Programs." *California Healthline.* January 31, 2014. http://www.californiahealthline.org/articles/2014/1/31/cms-data-show-mixed-results-from-medicare-aco-programs

9 "CBS News, New York Channel 7, 7/17/15" *Seen at 11: A Phone Call From Collectors That Can Actually Get You OUT Of Debt.* http://newyork.cbslocal.com/2015/07/17/seen-at-11-a-phone-call-from-collectors-that-can-actually-get-you-out-of-debt/

Chapter 5

1 Terhune, Chad. "California Fines Top Health Insurers for Overstating Obamacare Networks." *The Los Angeles Times,* November 3, 2015. http://www.latimes.com/business/healthcare/la-fi-obamacare-network-probe-20151103-story.html

2 Norris, Louise. "Just how bad are junk health policies?" HealthInsurance.Org. January 10, 2014. http://www.healthinsurance.org/blog/2014/01/10/just-how-bad-are-junk-health-policies/

3 "CMS Data Show Mixed Results from Medicare ACO Programs" *California Healthline.* January 31, 2014. http://www.californiahealthline.org/articles/2014/1/31/cms-data-show-mixed-results-from-medicare-aco-programs

4 "CBS News, New York Channel 7, 7/17/15" *Seen at 11: A Phone Call From Collectors That Can Actually Get You OUT Of Debt.* http://newyork.cbslocal.com/2015/07/17/seen-at-11-a-phone-call-from-collectors-that-can-actually-get-you-out-of-debt/

Chapter 6

1 *The Debt Collection Racket in New York: How the Industry Violates Due Process and Perpetuates Economic Inequality.* New Economy Project. June 6, 2013. http://www.neweconomynyc.org/resource/one-resource/

2 Bovee, Michael. "Arrow Financial Services – Debt Buyer Closed Shop – Debts Purchased – LVNV Collecting" *Debt Relief and Credit Guides.* November 5, 2012. http://consumerrecoverynetwork.com/arrow-financial-services-debt-buyer-closed-shop-debts-purchased-lvnv-debt-collection/

3 Gloomylunatic. "Debtors' Prison Returns in the US." *DiscloseTV.* June 19, 2010. http://www.disclose.tv/action/viewvideo/47957/Debtors__Prison_Returns_in_the_US/

4 cwalters. "'I Stopped Denying People': Ex-Bank Of America CSR Tells All." *Consumerist.* November 27, 2009. http://consumerist.com/2009/11/27/ex-bank-of-america-employee-tells-all-in-youtube-video/

5 "Delta Management Associates Donates more than $50,000 to Charity through 2013." *InsideARM.com.* January 13, 2014. http://www.insidearm.com/daily/debt-collection-news/debt-collection/delta-management-associates-donates-more-than-50000-to-charity-through-2013/; "ARM Firm Monarch Recovery Announces Charity Program Monarch Cares."

InsideARM.com. September 19, 2012. http://www.insidearm.com/daily/debt-collection-news/debt-collection/arm-firm-monarch-recovery-announces-charity-program-monarch-cares/;

"RevSpring Collects Toys and Canned Food for Charity" *InsideARM.com*. December 30, 2013. http://www.insidearm.com/daily/collection-technologies/collection-technology/revspring-collects-toys-and-canned-food-for-charity/

6 Lazare, Sarah. "1 in 3 Americans Have a Debt in Collections: Study." *Common Dreams*. July 19, 2014. http://www.commondreams.org/news/2014/07/29/1-3-americans-have-debt-collections-study

7 Health Insurance Portability and Accountability Act. *Wikipedia*. http://en.wikipedia.org/wiki/Health_Insurance_Portability_and_Accountability_Act

8 "Dealing with Debt from Medical Expenses." Allegheny County Bar Association. http://www.acba.org/yldlgfmc/Dealing-with-debt-from-medical-expenses

9 Strike Debt website. www.StrikeDebt.org.

10 Debt Collective website. www.DebtCollective.org.

11 Renter, Elizabeth. "Will FICO 9 Fix My Medical Debt?" *Nerd Wallet*. August 20, 2014. http://www.nerdwallet.com/blog/health/2014/08/20/fico-9-fix-medical-debt/

12 "FICO Score 9 Introduces Refined Analysis of Medical Collections." FICO. August 7, 2014. http://www.fico.com/en/about-us/newsroom/news-releases/fico-score-9-introduces-refined-analysis-medical-collections/

13 Konsko, Lindsay. "Medical Bills on Your Credit Report: Everything You Need to Know." *Nerd Wallet*. August 19, 2014. http://www.nerdwallet.com/blog/health/2014/08/19/medical-bills-on-credit-report/

14 Andtriotis, Annamaria. "Credit-Reporting Giants Agree to Overhaul." *The Wall Street Journal*. March 9, 2015. http://www.wsj.com/articles/credit-reporting-giants-agree-to-overhaul-1425873884

15 "CBS News, New York Channel 7, 7/17/15" *Seen at 11: A Phone Call From Collectors That Can Actually Get You OUT Of Debt*. http://newyork.cbslocal.com/2015/07/17/seen-at-11-a-phone-call-from-collectors-that-can-actually-get-you-out-of-debt/

Chapter 7

1 Bell, Michael. "Why 5% of Patients Create 50% of Health Care Costs." *Forbes*. January 10, 2013. http://www.forbes.com/sites/michaelbell/2013/01/10/why-5-of-patients-create-50-of-health-care-costs/

2 "Care of Chronic Illness in Last Two Years of Life." *The Dartmouth Atlas*. http://www.dartmouthatlas.org/data/topic/topic.aspx?cat=1

3 "IOM Report: Estimated $750B Wasted Annually In Health Care System." *Kaiser Health News*. September 7, 2012. http://khn.org/morning-breakout/iom-report/

4 Himmelstein, David U., Miraya Jun, Reinhard Busse, Karine Chevreul, Alexander Geissler, Patrick Jeurissen, Sarah Thomson, Marie-Amelie Vinet, and Steffie Woolhandler. "A Comparison Of Hospital Administrative Costs In Eight Nations: US Costs Exceed All Others By Far." Abstract. *Health Affairs*. http://content.healthaffairs.org/content/33/9/1586.abstract

5 Grube, Mark, Kenneth Kaufman, and Robert York. "Decline in Utilization Rates Signals a Change in the Inpatient Business Model." *Health Affairs Blog*. March 8, 2013. http://healthaffairs.org/blog/2013/03/08/decline-in-utilization-rates-signals-a-change-in-the-inpatient-business-model/

6 Gottfried, Dennis. "Too Many Doctors, But Too Few Primary Care Ones." *The Huffington Post*. May 10, 2010. http://www.huffingtonpost.com/dr-dennis-gottfried/too-many-doctors-but-too_b_568703.html

7 Ibid.

8 *How Is a Shortage of Primary Care Physicians Affecting the Quality and Cost of Medical Care?* American College of Physicians. 2008. http://www.acponline.org/advocacy/current_policy_papers/assets/primary_shortage.pdf

9 Brownlee, Shannon, and Vikas Saini. "Bigger Hospitals Mean Higher Prices, Not Better Care." *Bloomberg View*. February 18, 2014. http://www.bloombergview.com/articles/2014-02-18/bigger-hospitals-mean-higher-prices-not-better-care

10 "Hospital Outpatient Prices Much Higher than Community Settings for Same Services." National Institute for Health Care Reform. June 26, 2014. http://www.nihcr.org/news_Hospital-Outpatient-Prices

11 "AHA: Hospitals' Economic Contribution Often Overlooked." *AHA News*. Jan 25, 2013. http://news.aha.org/article/aha-hospitals-economic-contribution-often-overlooked

12 "CBS News, New York Channel 7, 7/17/15" *Seen at 11: A Phone Call From Collectors That Can Actually Get You OUT Of Debt.* http://newyork.cbslocal.com/2015/07/17/seen-at-11-a-phone-call-from-collectors-that-can-actually-get-you-out-of-debt/

Chapter 8

1 "Charitable Care." Southern New Hampshire Health. http://www.snhhs.org/Charitable-Care

2 Fuscaldo, Donna. "Medical Bankruptcies are Still a Problem, Here's What to Expect." FOXBusiness. February 18, 2014. http://www.foxbusiness.com/personal-finance/2014/02/18/medical-bankruptcies-are-still-problem-here-what-to-expect/

3 Michon, Kathleen. "Debt Scavengers and Zombie Debt." Nolo. Undated. http://www.nolo.com/legal-encyclopedia/debt-scavengers-zombie-debt-32240.html

4 Douglas, Danielle. "Taking on the Country's Biggest Debt Buyer." *The Washington Post*. May 9, 2014. http://www.washingtonpost.com/business/economy/taking-on-the-countrys-biggest-debt-buyer/2014/05/09/fbd65a24-a94d-11e3-b61e-8051b8b52d06_story.html

5 "CBS News, New York Channel 7, 7/17/15" *Seen at 11: A Phone Call From Collectors That Can Actually Get You OUT Of Debt.* http://newyork.cbslocal.com/2015/07/17/seen-at-11-a-phone-call-from-collectors-that-can-actually-get-you-out-of-debt/

Chapter 9

1 Boyer, Ray, and Paul Colford. "National Survey: Privately Insured in America: Opinions of Health Care Costs and Coverage" Associated Press-NORC University of Chicago. October 13, 2014. http://www.apnorc.org/PDFs/Coverage/NORC-AP-NORC-Release-Privately-Insuredl.pdf

2 "CBS News, New York Channel 7, 7/17/15" *Seen at 11: A Phone Call From Collectors That Can Actually Get You OUT Of Debt.* http://newyork.cbslocal.com/2015/07/17/seen-at-11-a-phone-call-from-collectors-that-can-actually-get-you-out-of-debt/

Chapter 10

1 The website for Rolling Jubilee. http://RollingJubilee.org

2 Ashton, Jerry. "Reflecting on Rescuing Stranded Starfish and Abolishing Medical Debt." *The Huffington Post*. November 12, 2013. http://www.huffingtonpost.com/jerry-ashton/reflecting-on-rescuing-st_b_4261708.html

3 Saul, Heather. "Occupy Wall Street Buys $15m of Americans' Personal Debt in Rolling Jubilee Scheme." *The Independent*. November 13, 2013. www.independent.co.uk/news/world/americas/occupy-wall-street-buys-15m-of-americans-personal-debt-in-rolling-jubilee-scheme-8936969.html

4 Madrak, Susie. "The Rolling Jubilee Project Pays Off Round 2 Of Medical Debt." *Crooks and Liars*. November 13, 2013. "http://crooksandliars.com/susie-madrak/rolling-jubilee-project-pays-round-2

5 Andreou, Alex. "Occupy Wall Street's Debt Buying Strikes at the Heart of Capitalism." *The Guardian*. November 13, 2013. www.theguardian.com/commentisfree/2013/nov/13/occupy-wall-st-debt-buying-heart-capitalism

6 Henwood, Doug. "The Problem with (Strike) Debt." *Jacobin*. November 2012. https://www.jacobinmag.com/2012/11/the-problem-with-strike-debt/

7 Weber, Katherine. "'Rolling Jubilee' Cites Bible in Project to 'Forgive' Anonymous Debts." *Christian Post*. November 16, 2013. http://www.christianpost.com/news/rolling-jubilee-cites-bible-in-project-to-forgive-anonymous-debts-85115/

8 Lerner, Michael. "Sabbatical Year and Jubilee in Twenty First Century America." *Tikkun.* January 14, 2015. http://www.tikkun.org/nextgen/sabbatical-year-and-jubilee-in-twenty-first-century-america

9 Ashton, Jerry. "Jubilee and Debt Abolition: A Bill Collector's Perspective." *Tikkun.* February 18, 2015. http://www.tikkun.org/tikkundaily/2015/02/18/jubilee-and-debt-abolition-a-bill-collectors-perspective/

10 Solomon, Norman. "The Jubilee and the Global Economy: Lessons from Leviticus." *Tikkun.* Undated. http://www.tikkun.org/nextgen/the-jubilee-and-the-global-economy-lessons-from-leviticus

11 Lunsford, Patrick. "Debt Buyers May See Competition from Occupy Wall Street." *InsideARM.com.* November 9, 2012. http://www.insidearm.com/daily/debt-buying-topics/debt-buying/debt-buyers-may-see-competition-from-occupy-wall-street/

12 Ashton, Jerry. "Strange Bedfellows: Occupy Wall Street and the Bill Collector!" *The Huffington Post.* November 14, 2012. www.huffingtonpost.com/jerry-ashton/strange-bedfellows-occupy_1_b_2122400.html

13 RIP Medical Debt website. http://ripmedicaldebt.causevox.com/

14 "CBS News, New York Channel 7, 7/17/15" *Seen at 11: A Phone Call From Collectors That Can Actually Get You OUT Of Debt.* http://newyork.cbslocal.com/2015/07/17/seen-at-11-a-phone-call-from-collectors-that-can-actually-get-you-out-of-debt/

Chapter 11

1 Rubin, Rita. "Dialysis Treatment in USA: High Costs, High Death Rates." *USA Today.* August 23, 2009. http://usatoday30.usatoday.com/news/health/2009-08-23-dialysis_N.htm

2 "Health Care Employment as a Percent of Total Employment." The Henry J. Kaiser Family Foundation. May 2014. http://kff.org/other/state-indicator/health-care-employment-as-total/; "National Health Expenditure Data: Historical." Centers for Medicare and Medicaid Services. Last modified December 9, 2014. https://www.cms.gov/research-statistics-data-and-systems/statistics-trends-and-reports/nationalhealthexpenddata/nationalhealthaccountshistorical.html

3 Andre, Claire, Manuel Velasquez, and Tim Mazur. "Voluntary Health Risks: Who Should Pay?" *Issues in Ethics.* 6, no. 1. Fall 1993. http://scu.edu/ethics/publications/iie/v6n1/voluntary.html

4 Bader, Pearl, David Boisclair, and Roberta Ferrence. "Effects of Tobacco Taxation and Pricing on Smoking Behavior in High Risk Populations: A Knowledge Synthesis." *International Journal of Environmental Research and Public Health.* 8, no. 11. November 2011, 4118–4139. Published online, US National Library of Medicine, National Institutes of Health. October 26, 2011. http://www.ncbi.nlm.nih.gov/pmc/articles/PMC3228562/

5 "Healthcare Costs Rise from Smoking Population." *Bravo Wellness*. July 18, 2013. http://www.bravowell.com/healthcare-costs-rise-from-smoking-population/

6 Frazão, Elizabeth. "High Costs Of Poor Eating Patterns in the United States." *Agriculture Information Bulletin*. No. (AIB-750), May 1999, 494. http://www.ers.usda.gov/media/91018/aib750a_1_.pdf

7 "Genes and Human Disease." World Health Organization. http://www.who.int/genomics/public/geneticdiseases/en/index3.html

8 Singh, Deepa. "The Economic Costs of Environmental Health Impacts." *Environmental Factor.* July 2014. http://www.niehs.nih.gov/news/newsletter/2014/7/science-economic/index.htm

9 Wilson, Michael. "Pope Francis, in New York, Takes On Extremism and Inequality." *The New York Times*. September 25, 2015. http://www.nytimes.com/2015/09/26/nyregion/pope-francis-visits-new-york-city.html?emc=edit_th_20150926&nl=todaysheadlines&nlid=39361574&_r=0

10 Burke, Daniel. "Pope Calls Greed 'The Devil's Dung'." CNN.com. July 11, 2015. http://www.cnn.com/2015/07/07/world/pope-mass-ecuador-quito

11 Dias, Elizabeth. "The Possible Presidential Candidate Who Agrees the Most with Pope Francis." *Time*. January 9, 2015. http://time.com/3661552/bernie-sanders-pope-francis/

12 Fleetwood, Blake. "Donald Trump Channels Occupy Wall Street, and the Revolt Against the Ruling Elite." *The Huffington Post*. September 26, 2015. http://www.huffingtonpost.com/blake-fleetwood/donald-trump-channels-occ_1_b_8198404.html

13 Cha, Ariana Eunjung. "CEO Martin Shkreli: 4,000 Percent Drug Price Hike Is 'Altruistic,' Not Greedy." *The Washington Post*. September 22, 2015. https://www.washingtonpost.com/news/to-your-health/wp/2015/09/22/turing-ceo-martin-shkreli-explains-that-4000-percent-drug-price-hike-is-altruistic-not-greedy/

14 Angell, Marcia. *The Truth about the Drug Companies: How They Deceive Us and What to Do About It.* New York: Random House. 2005. Online. http://www.wanttoknow.info/truthaboutdrugcompanies

15 Rolley, Sam. "Bernie Sanders Wants to Take on Big Pharma." *Personal Liberty.* September 2, 2015. http://personalliberty.com/bernie-sanders-wants-to-take-on-big-pharma/

16 Zwahlen, Roy. "The Real Reason Why Salk Refused to Patent the Polio Vaccine." *Biotech Now.* http://www.biotech-now.org/public-policy/patently-biotech/2012/01/the-real-reason-why-salk-refused-to-patent-the-polio-vaccine-a-myth-in-the-making

17 Martin, Andrew. "Debt Collectors Cashing in on Student Loans." *The New York Times.* September 8, 2012. http://www.nytimes.com/2012/09/09/business/once-a-student-now-dogged-by-collection-agencies.html?page%20wanted=all&_r=0

18 Ashton, Jerry. "Campus Loan Predators: Get Out the Bait and Traps!" *Written Off: America and Americans*. August 11, 2010. Last updated October 20, 2011. http://writtenoffamerica.com/campus-loan-predators-get-out-the-bait-and-traps/

19 Ashton, Jerry. "America's Financial Institutions and Student Lenders — Attention: OWS 'Occupy Student Debt Committee' Has Something to Say." *The Huffington Post*. November 21, 2011. http://www.huffingtonpost.com/jerry-ashton/americas-financial-instit_b_1105224.html

20 Ashton, Jerry. "Occupy Abolishes Almost $4,000,000 in Student Debt, Enrolls Campus Activists, Announces Nationwide 'Debt Collective'." *The Huffington Post*. September 17, 2014. http://www.huffingtonpost.com/jerry-ashton/occupy-student-loan-debt_b_5833178.html

21 Debt Collective website. www.debtcollective.org

22 "Debt Relief for Students Snarls Market for Their Loans." National Association for Student Financial Aid Admissions. September 25, 2015. http://www.nasfaa.org/news-item/6015/Debt_Relief_for_Students_Snarls_Market_for_Their_Loans

23 Fineman, Melanie. "The Perils of Payday Loans." Religious Action Center of Reform Judaism. August 5, 2015. http://blogs.rj.org/rac/2015/08/05/perils-payday-loans/

24 Giusti, Autumn Cafiero. "The consumer perils of a car title loan." Bankrate. Undated. http://www.bankrate.com/finance/auto/consumer-perils-car-title-loan.aspx

25 Van Doren, Vanessa. "Future Doctors Rising Up for 'Medicare for All'." *Common Dreams*. September 24, 2015. http://www.commondreams.org/views/2015/09/24/future-doctors-rising-medicare-all

26 "CBS News, New York Channel 7, 7/17/15" *Seen at 11: A Phone Call From Collectors That Can Actually Get You OUT Of Debt.* http://newyork.cbslocal.com/2015/07/17/seen-at-11-a-phone-call-from-collectors-that-can-actually-get-you-out-of-debt/

Epilogue

1 "Rub-a-dub-dub" at All Nursery Rhymes. http://www.allnurseryrhymes.com/Rub-a-dub-dub.html

ABOUT THE AUTHORS

Robert E. Goff

With more than 40 years of experience in the healthcare industry, Robert E. Goff is a recognized expert in care delivery, organization and financing. His career has spanned a wide range of leadership positions as a hospital administrator, regulator, managed care executive, consultant and association executive. He has held an academic appointment as an adjunct professor, instructing in Managed Care and Healthcare Strategic Planning with the New School University, NY, and has been a frequent lecturer to physicians and community organizations.

Goff is the author of many articles and training materials for medical practices. Published works include "Managed Care, the Solution No One Wanted;" *Health Benefits Magazine,* Fall 1997 and Revenue Cycle Management for Physicians: & Editions 1–7, 2000–2010.

As an entrepreneur, he has been responsible for the development of numerous healthcare businesses, including one of the first for-profit HMOs in New York State, one of the earliest physician practice management companies, a chain of urgent care centers, the first network model Medicare and Medicaid managed-care plans in a secondary market, as well as a variety of provider based health care business initiatives.

Goff serves as Executive Director and CEO of University Physicians Network, LLC (UPN) in New York City, as well as a corporate director and advisor to healthcare businesses in both technology and care delivery.

Goff received his advanced education at Northeastern University, Babson College, and Cornell University. He resides in Dutchess County, NY.

Jerry Ashton

Jerry Ashton is a veteran in the credit and collections industry who, over the past 40+ years, has become the industry's acknowledged gadfly and critic of its excesses and missteps. Starting out in 1978 as a door-to-door salesman for a fledgling fixed-fee collection agency called Transworld Systems, he advanced to East Coast Regional Sales Manager overseeing the efforts of hundreds of salespeople and millions of dollars in annual revenue.

In 1995, dissatisfied with the way he perceived debtors to be treated, he founded CFO Advisors, Inc. and set out to develop customer-centric approaches to accounts-receivable controls. His specially trained teams, on and off-site, at one point regularly serviced more than a half-billion dollars annually in receivables in several states for clients that included Johnson & Johnson, Hearst and Gannett newspapers, RR Donnelley, Snelling and Snelling, and Biosense Webster.

In addition to his writing credit/collection-oriented articles for industry publications such as *Credit Today, Financial Manager* and *InsideARM,* he has delivered internal workshops for Fortune 500 corporations and served as a guest speaker for industry associations as well as chaired international credit conferences. He has been quoted on the front page of the *New York Times* and had his work featured in *YES! Magazine, Tikkun* and *The Nation.*

Ashton shuttered CFO Advisors after a successful 14-year run and came out of semi-retirement in 2011 to chronicle adventures of Occupy Wall Street. Inspired by the movement's brief foray into abolishing medical debt by way of its "Rolling Jubilee" working group, in 2014 he co-founded RIP Medical Debt to expand on that goal as a 501(c)(3) not-for-profit organization.

He resides in New York City.

INDEX

32649712R00132

Made in the USA
Middletown, DE
12 June 2016